Also by Rob Neto

Non-fiction

Sidemount Diving The Almost *Comprehensive Guide*

Sidemount Diving translations

Buceo Sidemount (Spanish)
Sidemount Duiken (Dutch)
Sidemount Tauchen (German)

Fiction

Beyond the Grate
Into the Darkness Beyond
Beyond Hope
Beyond the End of the Line

Adventure series

Beneath the Jungle of Cozumel: Connecting the Crowns
The Hidden Rivers of Florida: Discoveries

Recreational Sidemount Diving

The *Not So* Comprehensive Guide

ROB NETO

Photography by Laurent Miroult

All diving activities have inherent risks involved. Each individual diver engaging in any form of diving must accept the risks and accept the responsibility for their own actions. The author and publisher assume no liability to anyone for loss, damage, injury or death caused by any error or omission in these works. Any and all such liability is disclaimed. The information in this manual pertains to utilizing sidemount diving equipment, and is only to be used as a supplement to recognized training by a qualified sidemount instructor from an internationally recognized training agency. This text assumes the reader has a basic knowledge of scuba diving and should not be used to replace professional instruction and good judgement on the part of the diver.

Cover Photo: Author Rob Neto above a reef in Cozumel, Mexico by Laurent Miroult

Back Cover Photos: Jennifer Neto above a reef in Cozumel, Mexico by Laurent Miroult / Author Rob Neto checking out a cave entrance in the Florida panhandle by Jennifer Neto

Book design by Rob Neto

Printed in the USA

ISBN: 9781961612204

DEDICATION

To those divers who just want to have fun with some tanks on their sides.

ACKNOWLEDGEMENTS

This book is a result of more than two decades of trial and error experimenting with different methods and configurations in sidemount. When I first started diving sidemount there was only one training agency that offered a basic sidemount class and finding an instructor that taught that class was next to impossible. After a few years of diving sidemount and tweaking gear, I began teaching it myself. Over the next few years I continued to learn and refine my approach to sidemount based on different issues I encountered with my students. So my first thanks goes to all of my students over the years who have helped me grow as a sidemount diver. Many of the needs they had – cold water diving, boat diving, diving with various sidemount rigs and various size cylinders – have allowed me to expand my knowledge through them. It forced me to develop solutions for their needs. And you'll find many of those solutions in this book. Before continuing with acknowledgements. I want to put it out there that any and all mistakes, whether grammatical or technical, are on me. Although I had several people proof my book I am responsible for the final product.

To continue, I want to thank my wife for her support throughout this project. I have spent countless hours researching, writing, obtaining photographs, and designing this book. Thanks for also being a model in some of the photos and a photographer of others. Many thanks also go out to Oliver Albrecht for reading and critiquing several editions of the text and providing valuable feedback. Oliver deserves acknowledgement for allowing me to use some photographs he took and helping me get some additional photographs during our dives together. Thanks to Laurent Miroult for allowing me to use his wonderful photography for the cover design and many of the photos at the beginning of the chapters as well as throughout the book. He is a fantastic photographer! Also thanks to Laurent for the humbling foreword in the edition. Thanks to Jeff Bauer for providing feedback on earlier editions and guidance with the publishing process. Thanks to Doug Ebersole, Kelly Koesis, Mike Pedersen, and Toddy Waelde for their contributions of some of the photos used in this book. A huge thank you to Joel Silverstein for providing me valuable feedback and technical guidance during the creation of this book. He has been a great mentor for many years and helped me grow immensely as a diver. I also thank him for contributing the humbling foreword for the 1st edition. Finally, thanks must go out to you, the reader, for your support with this project.

FOREWORD

Of all the training I have had in diving, one has really helped me broaden my horizons, the one for sidemount diving. Its advantages are numerous. Among other things, it offers manageable redundancy, excellent stability in the water and streamlining, but also it allows access to places beyond the reach of other configurations. During my cave diving training, the choice of this system was quickly obvious. I was able to get the best out of it thanks to an outstanding sidemount and cave instructor, Rob Neto. To be a good instructor you must have the necessary knowledge but also a regular and intensive practice of what you teach, all seasoned with a good dose of passion. The thousands of hours spent underwater have provided Rob with invaluable experience, constantly seeking improvement and innovations, and this book is the result. Nothing will ever replace a teaching in the field, but this reference book will help you whatever your level might be: preparation to a course for beginners, discovery or review of certain points for the more experienced. Every sidemount diver should have this book in their library. I thank Rob for choosing a few of my photos to illustrate his work. They were made possible thanks to what I learned from him and the fantastic diving opportunities it was a privilege to share with him.

Laurent Miroult

CONTENTS

PREFACE

Since Jacques Cousteau first attached a converted air regulator onto a cylinder of compressed air divers have been grabbing cylinders, stashing them under their arms and jumping into the wonderful unknown alien environment we call the ocean. With the ease of a free diver, these explorers have found ways to carry their life sustaining breathing air with them underwater for more than eighty years. Today, divers use a plethora of methods to carry air with them underwater. This book explores the intricacies of a method of scuba diving known as sidemount diving. Sidemount diving is a streamlined, balanced, and efficient way to conduct scuba dives in most any environment without having to strap cylinders to a diver's back.

In 2015 I published the 1st edition of my sidemount diving book. Sidemount diving continued to evolve over the years. There are more sidemount systems available on the market. Sidemount courses are more prevalent. And there are new techniques that have been developed to make the art of sidemount diving more efficient. In response to that, I published the 2nd edition in 2020. More than twice the number of pages of the 1st edition, it introduced information and techniques that were not known or widely practiced in 2015. That edition goes into more detail in some areas and includes more than three times the photographs.

The original Sidemount Diving book has had great success over its first ten years. Not much changed since the release of the 2nd edition. While I've released a 3rd edition, that was mainly to make corrections of issues found while working on the Recreational Sidemount Diving book. I also added some information based on new techniques introduced since 2020, but that information isn't extensive. It is included in this book.

When I embarked on this project, I saw a need for a different type of sidemount diving book. The cost of printing the 2nd edition, a 300-page, full-color interior, results in a higher cover price. I wanted to offer a more affordable guide for those divers who want to learn better techniques for sidemount diving, yet aren't interested in the technical diving aspects. I wanted to offer a book that focused on recreational sidemount diving.

This book is essentially the same guide as the 3rd edition, minus all of the extraneous information that you don't need to know if you are only diving sidemount in open water over reefs with no decompression obligation. This book focuses on the recreational side of things. I've also added some information that's specific to recreational sidemount diving that's not included in the original guide.

This book is a culmination of years of experience diving sidemount around the world in a variety of settings and conditions. It's not intended to be an all-comprehensive book. With sidemount, that isn't possible because unlike other "styles" of diving, there is no standardization in sidemount diving. There are so many possible applications for sidemount and many divers are building their own sidemount rigs that even if someone could gather all of the information out there today, it would probably be incomplete tomorrow. And while I discuss the various types of sidemount systems available on the market, I don't review or mention every single one. Many of the systems available are similar enough in design that the principles mentioned in this book can be applied across the spectrum. This is the reason I only discuss sidemount systems by type rather than by manufacturer.

This book is simply a guide to sidemount diving. I have tried to cover as much information and as many applications as possible approaching it in a general sense. I've gone through this book and removed most of the references to cave diving to keep it open water focused. You will still find some information that can be traced to cave diving. It's impossible not to. After all, sidemount diving has its beginnings with cave divers. When sidemount first appeared, a majority of sidemount divers were cave divers. The population continued to grow. While at the beginning of the 2010s it was rare to see a sidemount diver at a dive site, it has become rare to see a backmount diver at some sites these days. Sidemount divers are even becoming more common on dive boats. I've gone on trips where my wife and I were the only sidemount divers on the boat and quite possibly on the island. That's not so much the case any longer.

Sidemount diving has been trending among open water circles. Most of the training agencies have added sidemount courses to their course offerings. And more and more non-overhead divers are showing an interest in sidemount diving. Some are flying across country to North Florida and down to the Riviera Maya of Mexico to learn from those who are considered the experts in sidemount diving. Many are also trying to learn on their own.

As prevalent as sidemount has become in recent years, it can still be difficult to find a *good* mentor or instructor in some locations. One of the purposes of this book is to help those divers who may not have good sidemount mentors or instructors available locally and cannot travel for the training. Whether you are new to sidemount or have years of experience, this book is meant to be a reference used to help all sidemount divers. It has even become the standard guide used by some instructors. This book is not a substitute for learning from a qualified mentor or taking a sidemount class with a qualified instructor, but it will hopefully supplement it.

And now for a short legal mumbo jumbo. Only qualified technicians should made modifications to scuba diving equipment. The modifications presented in this book are for your knowledge. If you decide to make any of these modifications, you do so at risk to yourself. The modifications should be completed by a service technician, or at the very least, the equipment should be inspected by one. The first dive following any modifications, regardless of who does them, should be in a controlled environment.

Now that that's done, sit back and enjoy the read. Hopefully you will learn something from this book. Visit our website at www.sidemountbook.com, and follow our Facebook page www.facebook.com/sidemount to see additional articles and photos on the topic of sidemount diving.

1 WHY SIDEMOUNT?

There are many reasons divers choose to dive in a sidemount configuration. The original reasons for diving sidemount were out of necessity (for a brief history of sidemount see chapter 16). While these reasons still hold true for many sidemount divers, the number of sidemount divers has grown quite a bit in the last decade and a half, and with that so have the reasons.

Let's face it, divers are getting older. Every morning when I wake up and have to get out of bed, my body tells me I'm no longer 20 years old. And this is much more pronounced now than it was 10 years ago when I released the first edition of The *Almost* Comprehensive Guide! While there are still many younger divers, scuba diving is not just a young person's sport. While there are divers of all ages, many are in the 40-60 year old range. At least the ones I tend to come across when we're out diving are in that age group. It makes sense. Training and gear are not cheap, and usually it takes getting settled into the workforce and life before one can afford to venture into scuba diving.

With age comes medical issues, specifically back and joint problems. After years of walking around dive sites and boats with more than 100 pounds of steel on your back, spines, knees, and ankles became less stable. This doesn't mean you should give up diving, especially when there are alternatives like sidemount!

Unfortunately, when sidemount diving was growing in popularity during the early 2010s, some people moved to sidemount diving simply because it looked *cool*. They may have thought they looked better in sidemount. They may have thought they looked like they were doing bigger, riskier dives in sidemount. It was about the appearance rather than the gear. It was just something to help boost the ego. This has also been an issue with backmounted doubles and in other sports outside of diving. Egos are everywhere. It's definitely not an issue unique to sidemount diving.

Walking heavy twinset cylinders gets more difficult as we age. Even a single cylinder can be difficult.

Poorly trimmed cylinders

These days it seems the popularity of sidemount has grown simply out of curiosity. As it becomes more prevalent around the world and more divers are exposed to it, those divers have their curiosity piqued. It's no longer so much about the look as it is about how effortless sidemount can seem once in the water. And, as we will see later, it truly is if set up properly. Don't get me wrong. There's a price to pay for that effortless feeling in the water. We'll discuss that later in the book.

Once someone has gotten in the water in a sidemount rig that has been trimmed out properly, the feeling of stability and freedom is one that's difficult to beat. Yes, there are people who have been in sidemount and didn't like it for one reason or another. Usually it's because they either tried it without a mentor or instructor to get them trimmed out correctly or because they were put in a rig that wasn't fitted to them or trimmed out properly.

Or maybe sidemount just wasn't for them. It's actually okay to not like sidemount. It's not for everyone!

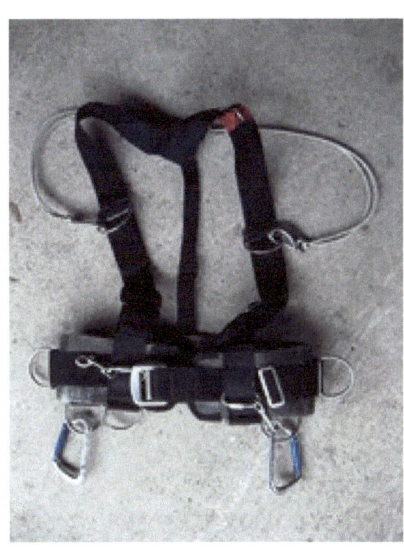

*Farr Sidemount Harness –
one of the original sidemount
harnesses*

*Dive Rite Nomad Sidemount
Rig – one of the original
commercial sidemount rigs*

So let's go back to the reason of necessity because that's how sidemount was born and why many people turn to sidemount. In the 1960s, early cavers in the United Kingdom began utilizing the sidemount method of diving in sumps, submerged sections of dry caves. Originally, the necessity was in having two redundant cylinders to conduct the dive in, but cylinders that were not attached to each other. While this could be done in independent backmounted cylinders, the additional hardware needed to mount cylinders on the back added to the load already being carried.

These sumps were often anywhere from hundreds of feet/meters to several miles/kilometers inside of a dry cave. Carrying manifolded cylinders isn't much fun when you have to do it from the back of your vehicle. Imagine having to carry them through hundreds of feet/meters (or more) of rocky, uneven, and sometimes low dry cave passage! Independent back-mounted cylinders were easier to carry; however, this configuration required additional clamps and equipment to properly mount them. Decreasing the required amount and weight of the gear was a necessity when it had to be carried a long distance into a dry cave.

Sumps were also not necessarily large enough to pass through with backmounted cylinders. While the entrance to the sump and most of the passage may have been large enough, restrictions were sometimes encountered that would require the removal of cylinders to pass through. Mounting cylinders along the side eliminated the need to remove them from the back, a dangerous practice.

This new configuration eventually made its way to the United States in the 1970s, specifically to North Florida. Cave exploration was at its peak and line was being placed in every passage found, except for the ones too small to get through. But even some of those were being explored by divers who were daring enough to remove their backmounted doubles and push them through ahead of themselves. Sidemounting cylinders made this dangerous practice unnecessary.

Armadillo Sidemount Rig – one of the original commercial sidemount rigs

Rigs were experimented with to use in the environment specific to North Florida. In the early uses of sidemount, submerged areas of dry caves were often short in distance and at shallow depths and didn't require much air volume. Also, getting the cylinders to the sumps necessitated choosing the smallest cylinders available and necessary for the traverse. In North Florida, the caves are completely submerged, average from 50-100 feet/15-30 meters in depth, and penetrate the earth for miles/kilometers. This required the use of larger steel cylinders that contained more breathing air and also required an air bladder to offset the negative buoyancy of the heavier steel cylinders.

Today, many of the larger passages have already been explored. The unexplored, virgin passages are either small or lie beyond small restrictions. Many divers are using sidemount now so they can access these smaller passages and continue exploration. And while some people may think sidemount divers are a little crazy for doing stuff like this, it's safer than methods previously employed - removing backmounted cylinders or rebreathers to push them through the

Narrow, steep path to a dive site in the south of France. Bonaire has a similar dive site access named 1000 Steps.

restriction ahead of the diver then having to put the rig back on. And then having to do the same thing on the return, but with limited or zero visibility! The lower profile of the configuration allows divers to negotiate passages with less clearance from floor to ceiling. The ability to reposition cylinders is also advantageous in negotiating passages that have minimal clearance from side to side. Unlike in backmounted cylinders and rebreathers in which the entire rig must be removed, in sidemount a cylinder can be moved forward by unclipping a single bolt snap. In other words, sidemount divers can get through smaller passages without completely removing any gear!

Not all divers who dive sidemount are cave divers who are interested in going into small passages. Some are recreational divers who simply want to get the 50-100 pounds/22-45 kilograms or more of weight off their backs. Diving a backmounted twinset, for the most part, requires gearing up at a table, stand, or rear of a vehicle and then walking to the water, sometimes several hundred feet/meters along narrow and sometimes steep, rocky paths for those of you who have visited Bonaire. Even a single backmounted tank requires either sufficient strength to lift the buoyancy compensator (BC) and tank onto your back, to have a buddy lift it onto your shoulders, or knees flexible and legs strong enough to bend down and then stand back up with an additional 45 pounds/22 kilograms hanging from your back. Sidemount cylinders, on the other hand, are best donned in the water. This means you can carry one tank at a time to the water before you don your BC.

Carrying one cylinder at a time is much easier on the back and knees than carrying a cylinder or two on your back. Even if a diver carries two cylinders to the water at the same time, holding the cylinders by the valves provides a more stable center of gravity than carrying them on the back. However, this may not be of any benefit to your back or knees.

When compared in the water, sidemount can be a more stable

configuration than backmount, especially with steel cylinders. Sidemount moves the mass of the weight alongside and lower on the body. In backmount, the weight mass is high and on the back. Rolling slightly to one side or the other causes the weight to take over the momentum and can flip the inexperienced diver over. In sidemount, a slight roll does nothing to stability. The cylinders balance each other out so there is no flipping over. This is basic physics. Think of flying a remote control helicopter versus a drone. A helicopter is much more difficult to control and maintain steadily in the air because it only has two rotors – one large one on top and a smaller vertical one on the tail. A drone, with four rotors, allows us to not only hold it steady in the air to get great photos and video, but it also allows us to do neat tricks like loop de loops without crashing. This is also possible in sidemount! You can flip yourself upside down and even swim upside down in sidemount! Something that's not so easy in backmounted cylinders.

There is also an increased safety factor in sidemount. Not only is the risk of losing all of one's air decreased with two independent cylinders, but the sidemount diver can see the cylinder valves and 1st stages. There's no guesswork as to where air is escaping from your cylinder. It's even safer than diving a backmounted twinset. Seeing where the leak is coming from eliminates the biggest risk factor of valve shutdowns present in backmounted cylinders. The leak can be seen and the cylinder supplying air to that regulator can be closed immediately, unlike in backmount in which the source of the leak usually has to be guessed, and then the isolator valve, along with the suspected side of the leak must be shut down. And if that doesn't stop the leak, the other valve must be shut down. Okay, we're not talking a lot of time or air loss, but in a true emergency, every breath counts. This is especially true if you're diving in a area with lots of boat traffic and must surface along an anchor line.

Carrying aluminum 80 cylinders on a narrow, rocky path to a dive site in Mexico

As is evident, there are several reasons for diving sidemount. Whether it's to advance your level of diving, because you're getting older and feeling it in your back, knees, and ankles, curiosity, or even to look cool, it doesn't matter. Whatever your reason for wanting to dive sidemount, this book will help you choose the right sidemount rig and customize it for your diving.

Diving the C-53 wreck in Cozumel, Mexico

2 CHOOSING A SIDEMOUNT RIG

Armadillo

Razor with Dive Rite Trim Pillow for buoyancy control

What sidemount system should you buy? That depends on a few factors. There are lots of choices in commercially produced sidemount rigs on the market today. When sidemount first started becoming popular there were only two options. Now many manufacturers have their own version of a sidemount rig. Some manufacturers even have a few different sidemount rigs available. With all of these choices available, how do you make a decision??

That can be a difficult question to answer. Fortunately, most sidemount systems fall into one of three categories. The differences among the rigs in those categories typically have to do with the wing – the rated lift and position of inflator and exhaust ports. Some manufacturers have tried to make their systems stand out with various options as well. So the first thing you need to do is decide which category of sidemount system you would like and then begin comparing rigs within that category.

Sidemount diving can be a very individual thing. What works for one person may not work for another. No matter what, the main question to ask yourself is what cylinders will you be using during most of your sidemount diving. This may help you decide which category to begin looking at and may also help decrease the number of choices within that category. There are rigs that are designed specifically for diving with aluminum cylinders and rigs designed specifically for diving with steel cylinders. Many manufacturers claim their rigs can be used with either type of cylinder, and while this may be true, these rigs are not optimal with either. While it used to be easy to figure out which rig was designed for aluminum and which for steel just by finding out how much lift the wing had, that isn't the case anymore.

As with any successful business, dive manufacturers want their products to appeal to the largest consumer market possible. There's nothing wrong with that. It's sound business practice. The problem is that there isn't one sidemount rig that is perfect for all diving conditions. Even though rigs tend to be marketed toward a type of cylinder, it's really not just about diving aluminum or steel cylinders. It's also about what exposure protection you're wearing. So which is more of a factor? Is it cylinders or exposure protection? Read on…

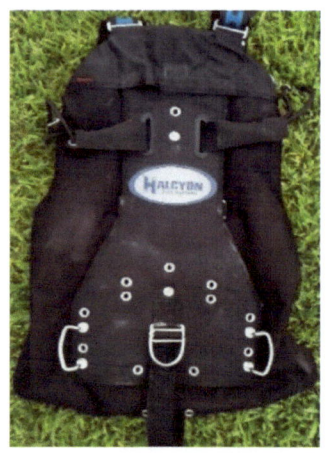

Halcyon Contour

Before we get too much into this, we need to discuss the purpose of a wing. The traditional name for these in the recreational diving world is buoyance compensator/control devices or BCDs. Moving into the technical world of diving, in which sidemount was first classified, the term BCD was dropped and the term wing was adopted. We must keep in mind that the change in name doesn't change the purpose of the equipment. A wing is still a buoyancy compensating device. Its purpose is to compensate for buoyancy changes during the dive.

Buoyancy changes occur in two ways. First, there is change in depth. As you descend deeper in the water column, the neoprene in your wetsuit or the air in your dry suit compresses with the increased pressure. In order to compensate for this compression, you must add air to the BCD/wing to maintain neutral buoyancy. The second change occurs as you breathe the air in your cylinders. Compressed air does have a weight. Aluminum cylinders will shift in buoyancy by 4 lbs/1.8

kg from full to empty. Steel cylinders can shift anywhere from 4 lbs/1.8 kg to 10 lbs/4.6 kg from full to empty. This is the buoyancy shift per cylinder! Double that for a set of two sidemount cylinders!

What does this mean for us as divers? Because at the end of a dive we may be anywhere from 8 lbs/3.6 kg to 20 lbs/9.1 kg lighter, this means we must carry enough lead weight to compensate for that change, making us that much over-weighted at the beginning of the dive. ***We want to be neutrally buoyant with empty cylinders!*** Some of you are probably thinking you never end a dive with empty cylinders, so you don't need that much weight. That's true…UNTIL something happens that prevents you from surfacing as planned and you and/or your buddy breathe your cylinders down to near empty. Do you really want to be struggling to maintain a safety stop or keep from surfacing into boat traffic after you've just had a major incident that drained your cylinders all while grossly underweighted? I certainly don't!

You need a wing that has the capability of keeping you neutral at the very beginning of the dive when you are over-weighted. Some of us are sinkers. Even with empty aluminum cylinders in a 5mm wetsuit, we sink to the bottom. This means we need to start with enough lift to keep us neutral at this point plus another 8 lbs/3.6 kg of lift to keep us neutral with full aluminum cylinders. Don't forget that neoprene compresses at depth, so we also need to add enough lift to compensate for the loss of positive buoyancy due to suit compression at depth. Sound complicated? Achieving neutral buoyancy has always been one of the most difficult skills in diving. I'll try to simplify it here.

Let's look at some specific examples. If you're wearing a dry suit with thick undergarments, no matter whether you're diving aluminum or steel cylinders, you will need enough weight to make you neutrally buoyant with near empty cylinders. With aluminum cylinders, you need to add more weight than with steel cylinders since aluminum weighs less than steel making aluminum cylinders less negatively buoyant. However, this isn't always the case. You need to consider the buoyancy characteristics of the cylinders you are diving.

Aluminum and steel cylinders range in buoyancy when empty from 7.7 lbs/3.5 kg negative to 4.4 lbs/2.0 kg positive. An aluminum 80 cf/11 L cylinder and a steel LP 120 cf/20 L cylinder both share the latter of those numbers: 4.4 lbs/2.0 kg positive when empty. The difference comes in the buoyancy characteristics when full. That same 80 cf/11 L cylinder is only 1.4 lbs/0.6 kg negative when full, while the steel LP 120 cf/20 L cylinders is 4.5 lbs/2.0 kg negative (this doesn't account for overfills). Overall, you will still need the same amount of weight to achieve that neutral buoyancy with empty cylinders. With full LP 120 cf/20 L steel cylinders, you just have more air weight in them that needs to be counteracted with the wing. As you breathe the air from the cylinders, you need less air in the wing. The only time the wing should be completely empty is when your cylinders are completely empty.

The type of suit you wear also affects your buoyancy. Wetsuits provide some positive buoyancy. The thicker the suit, the more positively buoyant you will be. If you are wearing a 3mm wetsuit. you won't need as much weight to counteract the neoprene as if you are wearing a 7mm wetsuit. If you are wearing a trilaminate dry suit with thick undergarments, you may find you can't get yourself under the surface of the water without lots of additional lead, even with all the air squeezed out of it. I personally can dive in an 8mm wetsuit using AL80 cylinders in brackish water with only 2 lbs/0.9 kg of additional weight. (Yes, I'm a sinker.) And I know people that require more than 30 lbs/14 kg of weight when diving in a dry suit and steel cylinders while I can dive a similar configuration using only 10 lbs/4.5 kg of additional weight. The only way to find out where you fit along that range is to get in the water and experiment.

First, see how much weight it takes to sink with only your wetsuit or dry suit. Then add your sidemount rig and near empty cylinders. Start with about 1000 psi/70 bar in each cylinder and get neutral. Depending on the cylinder you are using, the additional weight you'll need to be neutral with empty cylinders will be 2-3 lbs/1-2 kg. Look up the buoyancy characteristics for your cylinders and divide the buoyancy pressure by the buoyancy difference and that will tell you how much pressure equals how many pounds or kilograms.

Let's get back to choosing a sidemount rig. The determining factor for whether you need a 60 lb/27 kg lift wing or a 15 lb/7 kg lift wing comes down to your physical attributes and what you are wearing. The buoyancy characteristics of the cylinders plus the additional weight needed to maintain neutral buoyancy with empty cylinders only provide a starting point. Add the characteristics of your exposure protection and you can calculate how much lift you'll need.

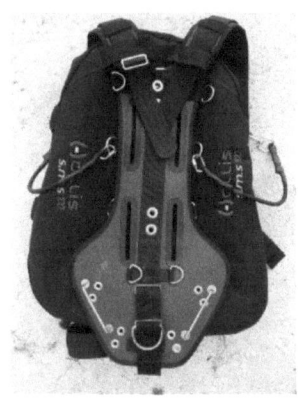

Donut shape wing (Hollis SMS100)

Horseshoe shape wing (Dive Rite Nomad)

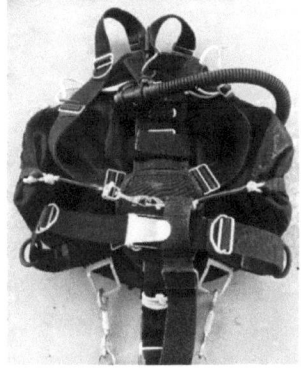

Hybrid shape wing (XDeep Stealth)

Divers that dive colder waters tend to use more lift, especially if they are diving in a wetsuit with steel cylinders. The compression of the wetsuit at depth eliminates some of the positive buoyancy and requires you to compensate with a wing. Divers that dive in warmer waters with thinner wetsuits can get away with less lift because the suits they are wearing aren't that buoyant to begin with, so there's less buoyancy loss. It also happens that divers in colder waters tend to use steel cylinders and divers in warmer waters tend to use aluminum cylinders.

What if you dive both? Then what do you do? The safe thing to do is go with the greater lift. You can avoid filling the wing all the way, but you can't get more lift out of a 15 lb/7 kg wing than 15 lbs/7 kg. Or you could end up like me and own three different sidemount systems, all which serve their own purpose! I use a horseshoe shaped wing with 35 lbs/16 kg of lift when diving in a dry suit with steel cylinders, a pillow shaped wing also with 35 lbs/16 kg of lift when diving a thick wetsuit with multiple aluminum 80 cf/11 L cylinders, and a pillow shaped wing with 10 lbs/4.5 L of lift when diving a rash guard with one aluminum 80 cf/11 L cylinder.

Why would I need 35 lbs/16 kg of lift if the air in my cylinders only weighs 16 lbs/7 kg? Because I often dive with stage cylinders which add even more weight. We'll discuss the shapes of wings briefly in the next paragraph and then in more detail in chapter 7. The sidemount rigs being manufactured all have their own purposes and work for someone. You need to figure out which one works for you. And if none of them do, make your own!

One of the main differences seen among the sidemount rigs with more lift (greater than 30lbs/13.5kg) is shape. Some wings are donut shaped, others are horseshoe shaped, and still others are pillow shaped. There's even a hybrid wing. What does this mean and how does it affect your diving?

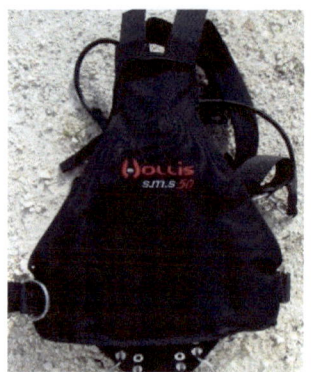

Pillow shaped wing (Hollis SMS50)

Donut shaped wings are, well, shaped like donuts. They are circular with a hole in the center and allow air to move completely around the wing. The advantage of this is that air is distributed around the periphery of the rig and when you're exhausting air from the wing, the air does not have to travel from two different locations to the exhaust valve. It can travel the shortest path from wherever it is in the wing.

Horseshoe wings are shaped like an upside down U. They also distribute air around the periphery. However, the air may not necessarily be able to be exhausted as easily as with a donut shaped wing. If you have an exhaust valve on one end of that U, then you need to move in such a way that the air from the other end of the U can travel around the top of the wing and back down to the other end in order to exhaust. Having an exhaust on the shoulder at the top helps alleviate this issue.

Pillow shaped wing (Dive Rite LT)

Pillow shaped wings, like pillows, come in various shapes and sizes. The common characteristic is that, unlike the other two types of wings, air is not distributed around the periphery. There is no center "cut-out". The air has unrestricted movement inside of the entire wing. It doesn't have to travel around the circumference of the wing. Rather, it can move anywhere along the wing to the exhaust valve. This makes dumping air easier in most situations.

All wings are typically designed so the greater lift is lower along the back and will help offset the heaviness in the feet that is common with sidemount. In the donut shaped wings, the lower part of the donut is usually fatter and wider. In the horseshoe shaped wings, the ends of the U are wider. While in the pillow shaped wings, the wing is typically shaped like a trapezium with the wider part lower and the wing secured to the harness closer to the waist than the shoulders.

Fully inflated donut wing. Notice how much it lifts the butt plate. Because the cylinders are attached to the butt plate, this also raises the bottoms of the cylinders at the beginning of the dive when they are full and heavier.

The disadvantage to the donut shaped wing is that the harness and butt plate are typically positioned above the wing, so when the wing is inflated, it will lift the harness and butt plate up away from the diver. If cylinders are being attached to the butt plate, this will also raise the bottoms of the cylinders and throw them out of trim. A simple solution should be to lengthen the leash, right? Wrong. Remember the discussion we had on buoyancy? As air is breathed from the cylinders, they become lighter and less air is needed in the wing. Less air in the wing means the butt plate won't be lifted as much away from the diver, so the cylinders will be positioned too low. Basically, at some point in diving with a donut shaped wing, it is likely that the cylinders won't be as perfectly trimmed out.

This doesn't affect things all that much, however. Many divers use donut shaped wings and the difference in marginal. Unless you're breathing your cylinders to less than 1000 psi/70 Bar, you should still have enough air in the wing to minimize the difference. This is usually only a factor with steel cylinders because they will have the larger weight shift. I'll discuss this in more detail in chapter 9.

The pillow shaped wings were originally designed for use with lighter cylinders, such as aluminums. They tend to have a single round or square shaped wing with the bottom being wider (trapezium) than the top. They are typically positioned above the waist strap and will not be underneath the attachment points of the cylinders. The consideration with these types of wings is how air is distributed in them and how much clearance they may require when full. MSR bladders tend to become somewhat football shaped (American football) creating a high profile when full. Whereas a wing with a baffle will be flatter. However, the baffled wing may have limited lift capacity. It's all a matter of give and take.

Another concern with pillow shaped wings involves physics. When comparing a donut or horseshoe shaped wing with a pillow shaped wing, you will achieve more lift with the former than with the latter. Underwater, trapped air will always rise. Place a sealed plastic bag in water and you can see the air rises to the center of the bag trying to lift it to the surface. All of the upward force is focused on that one location in the center of the bag. This is what happens with pillow shaped wings. Of course, we secure them to our harnesses and try to spread the upward force out over a larger area and even add baffles, but that only helps so much.

With donut and horseshoe shaped wings, the upward force is spread out over a larger area by nature of the design. The air can't rise to the center of the wing because there is no center. Forcing the air to spread over a larger area makes it more efficient. This is similar to aspect ratio in airplane wing designs. The higher the aspect ratio, the more efficient the flight. Or put more simply, the longer the wingspan compared to the width of the wing, the lower the lift-induced drag. In buoyancy wings, the more widely the lift can be distributed over the wing, the more efficient the lift will be. This is why I can use a wing with 35 lbs/16 kg lift with a set of steel LP 120 cf/20 L cylinders and multiple aluminum 80 cf/11 L stage cylinders, yet someone using a pillow shaped wing would typically need 45 lbs/20.5 kg or more of lift.

Hybrid wing (XDeep) - This design is a hybrid between a pillow and horseshoe shaped wing. The bottom of the U is at the lower back.

In a test in the pool using a 35 lb/16 kg lift horseshoe shaped wing sidemount rig, it took 30 lbs/13.5 kg of weight with the wing fully inflated to get the rig to be neutral. When taking the D-rings and other hardware plus the heavy duty webbing into consideration, that is very close to the actual rated lift of the wing. Doing the same test with a 28.6 lb/13 kg lift pillow shaped wing sidemount rig, it took 18 lbs/8 kg of weight to get the rig to be neutral. This rig had less hardware and webbing, as well as lighter webbing. So even when accounting for that, the wing still fell short by several pounds/kg of its rated lift capacity.

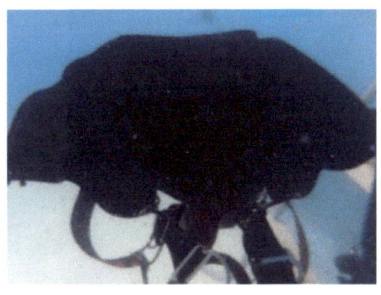

The pillow shaped wing was also much less stable in the water than the horseshoe shaped wing. If the weight was not evenly distributed on both sides of the pillow shaped wing, it would lean toward the heavier side, and even flip sideways at times. The horseshoe shaped wing could withstand 3 lbs/1.4 kg difference before it would lose its stability and lean slightly to the heavier side.

Fully inflated (above) and partially inflated (below) pillow shaped wing. Notice the fully inflated wing is flatter giving it a lower profile than the partially inflated wing. The partially inflated wing also has the majority of the air in the center of the wing, raising that above the sides.

A final style of sidemount rig we'll discuss is the Toddy Style sidemount system, in which a backplate is used as part of the harness. With this rig, a donut shaped wing is placed between two backplates on the harness. A standard backplate is positioned under the wing and a smaller backplate is placed over the wing. The backplates are held together with the use of sex bolts where the twinset bolts would typically insert. The shoulder webbing of the harness is woven through the slots at the top of the smaller, outer backplate and back into slots at the bottom of the larger, inner backplate and continue to form the waist strap. The crotch strap is woven through a slot at the bottom of the smaller, outer backplate.

The purpose of this rig is the added weight provided by the backplates, as well as versatility in being able to use it for backmount. One of the issues with sidemount rigs is where to mount weights. We discuss some of the options later in chapter 10. With this rig, much of the weight is able to be spread over the entire back. This can be useful if a majority of your diving is in cold salt water in a dry suit and you need the additional weight. However, if you are diving small swim-throughs in the warm water reefs, this may not be ideal for you. First, you likely don't need that much weight to make you neutrally buoyant. Second, because the backplates are not flexible, this rig can limit the types of swim-throughs you can penetrate as it can cause you to get wedged.

Toddy Style sidemount system. Larger plate is positioned on the inside against the back and the smaller (red) plate is on the outside of the wing providing additional weight as well as support for a backmounted twinset.

We've discussed lift and wing shape. The last thing I want to discuss is where the inflator and exhaust ports are located on the wing. With the horseshoe and donut shaped wings, you will usually have one port at the waist and one at the shoulder. Where they are exactly located depends on the rig. In sidemount with horseshoe and donut shaped wings, we typically want the inflator at the waist and the exhaust at the shoulder. Not all rigs come like this, but we'll discuss this modification in chapter 7. The one thing to make note of is whether the port is located above the wing (the side away from your back), or below the wing (the side against your back). This is important to know because it will affect the way you have to position yourself to exhaust air from the wing.

I've already mentioned that air rises in water. Any air that is in your wing will rise up against the top of the wing. To get that air out of an exhaust valve that is positioned on top at the shoulder, you simply have to raise your shoulder slightly higher than your waist and the air will travel along the top of the wing and out of the exhaust. If the exhaust port is against your back, the air can't escape your wing. It won't travel down to the port to get out of the wing. This means to get that port at the highest point, you have to orient yourself vertically. This may be acceptable to you. It's just something to keep in mind. We'll discuss more about the position of the ports later in the book.

The purpose of this chapter is to provide you with some basic information to consider when choosing a rig. The best way to make an informed decision is to find a mentor or instructor that has a variety of experience in several different conditions and rigs and have that person guide you in this process. But if someone tries to sell you on something as being the best all-around rig or method, turn around and run! There is no such thing!

Once you decide on a sidemount rig, you may have to size it properly. Most rigs come one size fits all these days, but others are sized according to shoulder pad length and webbing length. If you are considering a rig that has different size options, choose carefully. Unfortunately, it can be all too easy to end up with a sidemount rig that is too small. The sizes tend to run small, so don't buy a rig based on your shirt size.

This is probably the most difficult part of the process of becoming a sidemount diver. While in the early and mid-2000s, the decision regarding which rig to purchase was simple – you bought an Armadillo or a Nomad – many manufacturers have since jumped into the sidemount rig market. Some have done research and produce great rigs. Others have simply put a rig out there to get into the competition. Choose wisely!

3 CHOOSING YOUR CYLINDERS
AND SETTING THEM UP

Choosing your cylinders

Aluminum Cylinders

Many recreational sidemount divers choose to use aluminum cylinders. It's the most common cylinder available and the obvious choice. Aluminum cylinders are also the most common cylinder found when traveling. It's rare that you'll be able to find steel cylinders at tourist diving destinations. If you're interested in sidemount but not ready to spend money on new cylinders, you may want to try sidemount the first few times in aluminum cylinders because that's what you have readily available. Aluminum cylinders can be really great sidemount cylinders, especially for recreational scuba, but they cannot be treated like steel cylinders. Their buoyancy characteristics are completely different.

AL80 cf/11 L aluminum cylinder floating bottom after being breathed down

There are a few considerations when diving sidemount with aluminum cylinders. The most common aluminum cylinder, the 80 cf/11 L, will get positive as you breathe the air. The bottoms will start to float, and not just a little! There are a couple of options available to counteract this and keep the cylinders horizontal. Some divers choose to weight the 80 cf/11 L cylinders to make them negative and behave more like steel cylinders. This method was developed by divers who were used to diving steel cylinders and wanted similar cylinder characteristics when traveling where only aluminum cylinders were available. They use anywhere from a 2 lb/1 kg to 4 lb/2 kg weight threaded onto the cam band. This is enough weight to keep the cylinder from floating and usually enough to keep it from rotating (more on that later). The positioning of the weight is important. It must be located on the cylinder where it will be on the bottom when you are in a horizontal position so it keeps the cylinder positioned properly.

Weighted cam band. A 2 lb/1 kg weight is threaded onto the cam band and positioned so it is on the lowest point of the cylinder when in the water in a horizontal position.

While this may be an acceptable option for some sidemount divers, there is one thing to consider before implementing the use of weights on the cylinders. Obviously, the weights make the cylinders heavier. This makes it more difficult to get them in and out of the water. This could be a concern when diving from a boat.

Another method that's used by some is to unclip the bottom bolt snap of the cylinder from the butt plate or rear D-ring and clip it to a D-ring located on the side or front of the waist strap. This requires the second D-ring to be located in a position that holds the cylinder down so it cannot float. Some divers use a sliding D-ring on each side to adjust the position of the cylinders. This method works well when used in conjunction with the proper bungee method on the neck. One caution about sliding D-rings is that they can move along the waist strap without pressure applied to them. There are different variations of sliding D-rings, but they all seem to have the issue of sliding too freely. Sliding D-rings were in favor for some time, but they seem to have fallen out of favor more recently. I've also seen divers with a series of D-rings along the waist strap. As they breathe from the cylinders, they reclip the bolt snap to maintain their trim. The issues with this are that you now have a bunch of D-rings cluttering your waist strap and it creates a bit of task loading which can detract from the enjoyment of the dive.

Steel cylinders

LP 85 cf/12 L cylinders made by the same manufacturer.

The one on the left is shorter and fatter than the one on the right.

Don't make the same mistake one of my students made and buy one cylinder from one dealer and the other cylinder from a different dealer. To give him credit, he didn't know. The first dealer only had one cylinder in stock, so the student bought the second cylinder somewhere else. There's one problem with this. Not all cylinders are created equal! Just as with manifolded doubles, you must pair match sidemount cylinders. This is more of an issue with steel cylinders than it is with aluminums.

This student bought two cylinders both manufactured by the same company, but they were manufactured at different times. A quick glance at the cylinders showed them to look identical. Once in the water, it was obvious they were not. My student listed significantly to one side. Before I ever step foot in the water with my sidemount students, we spend a few hours setting up and customizing their sidemount rigs. This time was no different, so I knew it wasn't the rig. I made adjustments underwater to no avail. I then looked at the rig out of the water and adjusted things back to where they had been. I couldn't figure out what the issue was!

We went back to the water where we left the cylinders. They had started off with equal pressures. We had only been in the water for about five minutes, but they sat in the water differently. One was lying flat on the bottom and the other was at a 45 degree angle with the valve on the bottom! We pulled them out of the water to check the pressures – only about 100 psi/7 Bar difference. The 1st stages were the same as was the rigging on both cylinders. As we looked at them more closely, I discovered they had different manufacture dates. I also noticed that their shapes were slightly different, so slight that it was barely noticeable. One had more defined angles at the bottom and top of the cylinder than the other. Not only were they manufactured in different years, but they were different. This resulted in different trim characteristics. Lesson learned!

Now that you know to make sure your cylinders are from the same lot, you need to decide what steel cylinders to purchase. There's a lot more variety than with aluminum cylinders. An LP 85 cf/12 L is not the same regardless of manufacturer. You must choose your cylinders carefully because they all have very different buoyancy characteristics. Again, the type of diving you do can dictate which cylinders work best for you. Some people have no issues with any cylinders. Others cannot dive certain cylinders because of the change in buoyancy when the cylinders get to a certain air pressure.

The *galvanized* LP 85 cf/12 L cylinder is an all-around great cylinder for sidemounting. It is 7 ¼ inches/18 cm diameter. As you breathe from them, the buoyancy characteristics of the cylinders allow them to maintain horizontal trim. In other words, they don't shift position in the water. The more popular *painted* LP 85 cf/12 L cylinders, on the other hand, are designed differently and start to become bottom light when they get down to about 2200 psi/150 Bar. The lower the pressure, the lighter they get.

This isn't always an issue. The issue is more apparent when you use a bungee system that pulls on the handwheels of the valves causing them to rotate. As the cylinder

Full LP 85 cf/12 L cylinders. Note they are in-line with the diver.

Painted LP 85 cf/12 L cylinders with 2000 psi/140 Bar. Note the bottoms are starting to rise.

LP 85 cf/12 L cylinders with 1600 psi/ 110 Bar. Note the bottoms are rising significantly.

becomes lighter, the bungee loses some of its stretch and starts to pull up more on the valve. As this happens, the cylinder rotates on the lower attachment point, and this is ultimately what makes the cylinder appear to have a floating bottom. The bottom isn't actually floating. If it was doing that, we could simply move the clip to a D-ring on the front of the rig and be done with it. I mentioned that method in the section about aluminum 80 cf/11 L cylinders. If you do that with steel cylinders, they will hang below you rather than at your sides.

There are other bungee methods that can be used to prevent this from happening. It's a matter of personal preference. If you dive the painted LP 85 cf/12 L cylinders using the standard loop bungee method, you may end up with the bottoms of the cylinders floating above you, placing the cylinders out of trim during the latter half of your dive. We'll go more into bungee methods shortly.

Note the cylinder is not hanging from the leash, but rather pulling out from it.

Painted LP 95 cf/15 L cylinders with 1000 psi/70 Bar actually float.

Galvanized LP 95 cf/15 L cylinders may be good for some, but the general consensus from most people that have had them in the water is that they are heavy. If you need the additional weight, try them out. But most won't need that weight, or like it. However, painted LP 95 cf/15 L cylinders can be great for sidemounting. Because painted LP 95 cf/15 L cylinders are heavier and a couple of inches/few centimeters shorter than the LP 85 cf/12 L cylinder, it takes longer for the bottoms to get positively buoyant as described above. This usually doesn't happen until the pressure in the cylinders falls to around 1600 psi/110 Bar. If you plan on using these cylinders and breathing them below 1600 psi/110 Bar, you can expect the bottoms to not only begin rotating around and up as described a couple of paragraphs back if you use the loop bungee system, but they will also float.

Galvanized HP 100 cf/13 L cylinders are also great for sidemounting. Like the galvanized LP 85 cf/12 L cylinders, they have a 7 ¼ inch/18 cm diameter and hold their horizontal trim throughout the dive. There are some cylinders; however, that can end up being very bottom heavy. I've come across a few of these over the years. They aren't any specific brand or size. Sometimes it's just how that particular lot may have been manufactured. In those cases, it may be best to sell the cylinders to backmounters who will appreciate the heavier bottoms. I had one student that had a set of the heavier bottom steel cylinders and he couldn't get trimmed out until he had 12 lbs/5.5 kg of weight on his shoulders. I had another student that wouldn't trim out horizontally with even 16 lbs/7.25 kg of weight on his shoulders. The cylinders they had simply won't work for sidemount because they were much too bottom heavy.

Larger cylinders, such as LP 108 cf/17 L or LP 120 cf/19 L cylinders, may also work for some divers. These are large, tall, heavy cylinders and are not suitable for all sidemount divers. If you are less than 6 feet/180 cm tall, these may not be the cylinders for you. They will be too long and likely too heavy for you. They also require special considerations when rigging them up (more on that later). They fall somewhere in between the LP 85 cf/12 L and LP 95 cf/15 L cylinders in terms of when the bottoms begin to float.

These are just a few examples of some of the more common issues encountered with various cylinders. The examples provided are not intended to sway anyone away from purchasing a specific type of cylinder. What works or doesn't work for most sidemount divers doesn't mean it will work or not work for everyone. You don't know until you try it out. My recommendation is to get out there and try before you buy. And if you can, try the actual cylinders you intend to buy.

LP 95 cf/15 L on left LP 120 cf/19 L on right

In addition to the buoyancy characteristics, another consideration when choosing a set of cylinders for sidemounting is your height. As I mentioned a couple of paragraphs earlier, if you are 5'4"/160 cm tall, a set of LP 120 cf/19 L cylinders probably won't trim out well on you.

They're almost as tall as you! LP 120 cf/19 L cylinders are tall and will extend below the knees of someone that height. On the opposite end, if you are 6'6"/195 cm tall, a set of LP 95 cf/15 L cylinders probably won't trim out well on you either. They will only come down to your waist and cause you to be too head heavy. That aspect of choosing a set of sidemount cylinders isn't much different than when choosing a cylinder to carry in any other position.

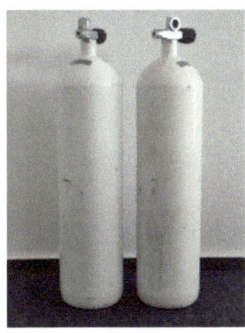

Concave bottom 12 L cylinders

Finally, a cylinder that is mainly found in Europe is the concave bottom 12 L cylinder. This cylinder is similar in dimensions to the LP 85 cf/12 L cylinders with rounded bottoms with the exception of the flat bottom with a concave indentation. These cylinders also have different buoyancy characteristics. As mentioned previously, the typical painted LP 85 cf/12 L rounded bottom cylinders tend to go out of trim as the air pressure decreases. This does not happen with the 12 L concave bottom cylinders. The concave cylinders are heavy enough on the bottom that they maintain their trim throughout the dive similarly to the galvanized LP 85 cf/12 L cylinders. These cylinders are great all around sidemount cylinders. Unfortunately, they are not readily available in the United States if that's where you reside.

We've discussed a variety of the more popular steel cylinders in use around the world. The most common cylinder you will come across in most locations is the painted LP 85 cf/12 L manufactured by Faber. Divers like them because they most approximate the shape and size of an aluminum cylinder, are easy to manipulate in the water, and are readily available. Although they do have some issues that can arise (no pun intended), these issues can be dealt with by using different methods of attaching them to your rig (we'll get into that later).

In the United States and occasionally in Europe, you will also come across people diving the painted LP 95 cf/15 L cylinders manufactured by Faber (these are my cylinders of choice). The buoyancy characteristics of these cylinders are more conducive to sidemount diving, and they also provide a little more air.

It's rare to see larger cylinders being used in sidemount, although not completely unknown to happen. I have a set of galvanized LP 108 cf/17 L cylinders and a set of painted LP 120 cf/19 L cylinders I use during certain dives. Those are more useful for technical overhead or decompression dives and outside the scope of this book.

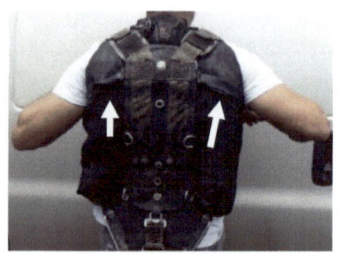

Old style innertube used to hold up sidemount cylinders

Neck Bungee Options

In the discussion of aluminum and steel cylinders, I've mentioned neck bungee methods. There are several options available to attach the neck of the cylinders to your sidemount rig. Some work better with certain cylinders so don't think you have to choose one and stick with it for all of your sidemount diving. Depending on the diving I'm doing, I use three of the methods that I'll discuss.

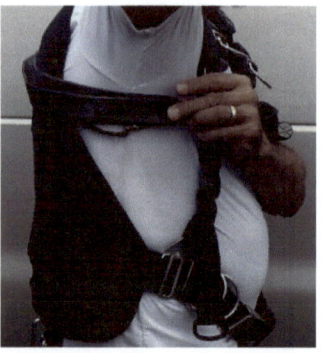

Old style innertube

One of the original methods employed by sidemount diving pioneers was the use of a bicycle innertube. At that time, standard recreational BCD jackets with modifications were being used instead of the modern-day harness and wing. Because those jackets typically didn't have any kind of attachment point around the chest or shoulders, it was necessary to create a method of holding the valves close to the body. They did this by using a bicycle innertube wrapped around the back and under the armpits. The valves were placed into the loops of the innertube and pulled up toward the body.

The first method to be used in a rig that was specifically manufactured by Dive Rite as a sidemount rig involved the use of thick bungee. Three-eighths inch/10 mm bungee

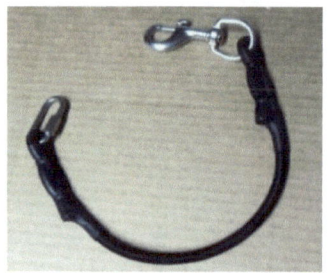

Dive Rite bungee system. The quick link secures to a small D-ring on the rear of the harness and the bolt snap secures to a chest D-ring. The bungee is wrapped around the handwheel of the valve.

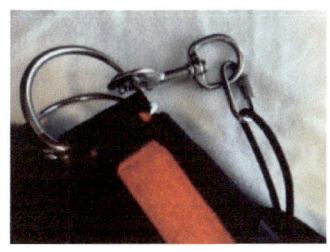

Bungee loop system. The bolt snap and quick link only serve to keep the loop from getting "lost" between the wing and the back of the diver.

Ring bungee system

Ring bungee system rigging on sidemount cylinder. The top bolt snap is secured to the valve with a choker and clipped to the ring.

was used to create a system with quick links and bolt snaps. The bungee was attached to small D-rings on the rear of the harness, routed under the armpits, and clipped to chest D-rings. The bungees were then routed around the handwheel portion of the valve to pull the valve close to the body.

Another method used was a bungee loop system. This method is similar to the innertube method just discussed. In the bungee loop system, the bungees are secured to the back of the harness, routed under the armpits, and end in loops. These loops are then placed over the handwheels of the valves to pull the valves up toward the body. A variation of this is to route the loops inside the valves, under them, and then over the handwheels so they are rotating the valves toward the center of the body. We'll discuss these variations in more detail in a later chapter.

There is also the ring bungee method that employs the use of a bit more hardware. Like the Dive Rite bungee (this is also a Dive Rite system), the bungees are attached to small D-rings on the back of the harness. Rather than a longer bungee that's clipped to a chest D-ring, this system uses a 2 inch/5 cm ring that's attached to the front end of the bungee. In order to use this method, you must also have compatible hardware on your sidemount cylinders to clip onto the ring. The ring bungee rigging on the cylinder includes a bolt snap at the neck of the cylinder. The bolt snap must be snugged to the neck of the cylinder and not remain loose. The bolt snap is then clipped onto the ring and the ring pulls the valve up toward the body.

This covers the most common neck bungee options in use today. There are variations on how each of these is used. We'll discuss them in detail in chapter 6.

Setting up your cylinders

You have your cylinders and you're ready to set them up. There are a couple of approaches to this. Any one of them works. You just need to find the best one for you. The most common method is using cam bands along the cylinders to attach the middle of the cylinder to a D-ring on the waist band or the rail on a butt plate. Cam bands work well and are great when you travel or if you use them on multiple cylinders. They are easy to remove and replace and last a long time. They are available in 2 inch/5 cm width or 1 inch/2.5 cm width. The 1 inch/2.5 cm width cam bands have a lower profile but require you to work the cam a little when you first place it on a cylinder. Otherwise, they can stretch in the water and slide easily up or down the cylinder if you're not careful. The narrow width of this material makes it more susceptible to stretching. The wider bands resist stretching.

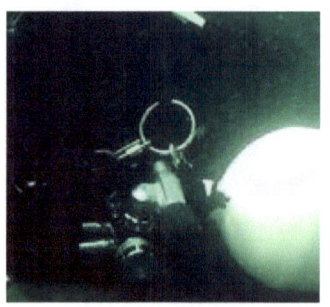

Choker and ring bungee. Note the choker holding the bolt snap on the cylinder neck.

Cam band

It doesn't matter where the buckle is placed on the cylinder as long as it doesn't interfere with the placement of the leash holding the bolt snap and doesn't interfere with how you tuck your long hose if you use one. Some divers will disagree with this and insist they need to go on the bottom or top of the cylinders or even on the sides. I have them in various positions on the cylinders I own and have never had an instance in which the location of the buckle made a difference in how the cylinders behave.

Some people choose to use worm gear clamps, commonly known as hose clamps. Worm gear clamps are less likely to slide along the cylinder

Double hose clamps

and can be quite stable. However, they aren't as easy to adjust or move from cylinder to cylinder, especially if you don't have a socket driver or screwdriver handy. If this is the way you choose to set up your cylinders, it is a good idea to double up the clamps for added strength. These clamps have been known to break. Having the redundancy of a second clamp can easily save a dive. If you do choose to use these clamps, be sure to use high grade stainless steel. Any other material will not do well with repeated exposure to water, especially salt water. You also want to use heavy duty cord or have tubing or a sleeve over the clamps. The movement of the cylinders can make the sharp edge of the clamp slice through the cord.

Cam bands hold the advantage when traveling if you will not be using the same cylinders every day because they are much easier and quicker to remove and apply. Hose clamps tend to be lighter and take up less space in your luggage. This may make the added time when using different cylinders each day worth it.

Whether you choose cam bands or worm gear clamps, you need to attach the cylinder to your rig somehow. The most common method is a bolt snap attached to the band or clamp with a leash. This leash needs to be made of a strong static nylon cord. The use of bungee instead of static cord may result in the bungee stretching and contracting based on the amount of air in the cylinder (because that determines the weight of the cylinder). Length will vary depending on your trim.

Some people also use carabiners to attach the cylinders to the rig. The carabiners are clamped directly in place rather than using a static cord. The use of carabiners can make trimming out the cylinders a little more challenging. With a leash, it's as simple as changing its length. With a carabiner, you will have to adjust the position of the D-ring on your waist strap or you may have to get a different size carabiner to get the cylinders trimmed properly.

The type of clips you choose to use on your rig is your decision. Use what works for you! Whether it's a butterfly clip or a large clip with a 1 inch/2.5 cm opening, it really doesn't matter. Adjustments can be made to make them all work. What will determine the best clip is where you dive. If you dive cold water and wear thick gloves, use the large clip. It will make a difference. If you choose butterfly clips, make sure to clip them with the opening down toward your waist so they do not become a line trap if you dive popular fishing sites.

Carabiner and Bolt Snap

Many divers will also place innertube around the cam band or worm gear clamp for various reasons. Cam bands have Velcro sewn onto them to secure the loose end of the webbing back onto itself. After repeated exposure to water, the Velcro begins to wear away or come off. Innertube keeps the loose end tucked in. I retired a set of cam bands that had close to 15 years of heavy use. The Velcro had come off completely after about eight years, but I was able to continue to use it for many years after. The only thing holding it against the cylinder was the innertube! I only retired them because the material was finally starting to tear. Innertube will also protect the cam buckle and keep fishing line from getting caught in the webbing or buckle. I've had students get caught up with line stuck between the Velcro of the webbing. With worm gear clamps, innertube also adds protection to the clamp and protects you and your exposure suit from sharp parts of the clamp.

Various clips – the large one is recommended for cold water.

Innertube

Most tires are tubeless these days, so where do you get these innertubes? They can be easy to find at many tire repair shops. There is a charge to these shops for disposal of rubber, so they usually have no problem with you taking innertube from their rubber pile. Your best chances of finding innertube are at a tire shop near a farming/ranching community, as many farmers and ranchers still have equipment that uses tires with innertube. Look for innertube with an inner diameter at least ¼ inch/7 mm smaller than the cylinder.

Now let's look at the attachment of the cylinder neck/valve to the rig. Some people choose to let the bungee hold the top of the cylinder in place. This can work; however, it doesn't provide redundancy. While it's not common for the valve to come out of the bungee, it can happen, especially if you're using thicker bungee. The hoses tend to keep the cylinder from going too far, but this places stress on the hoses if the cylinder neck falls out of the bungee. There is a simple method that can be used to provide some redundancy. Use an additional bolt snap on a length of static cord around the neck of the cylinder.

This also provides you with a third hand when you are putting your cylinders onto your rig in the water or walking across the boat to giant stride off the stern. The length of the cord on this clip needs to be long enough to not restrict how the cylinders rest along your side once the valves or necks are placed in the bungees. The bolt snaps should hang loosely from the chest D-rings.

Neck clip used to hold cylinder while donning and as redundancy for the bungee

If you choose to use the ring bungee system with a choker on the neck, the redundancy is missing from this method. Should the ring come loose from the bolt snap, the cylinder will hang from the hoses. Whatever method you choose, make sure it works for you and still allows you to properly trim your rig.

Choosing cylinders for diving sidemount can be a difficult task. Try as many different cylinders before making a final decision. Evaluate a variety of cylinders and choose one that works for you. You may decide you want multiple sizes for different types of diving. Don't be afraid to change things as your diving changes. You're expected to evolve as your knowledge and experience grow.

4 SETTING UP HOSES

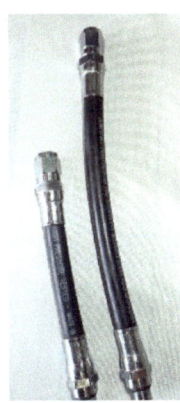

6 inch/ 15 cm & 9 inch/ 22.5 cm hoses

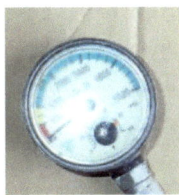

Plastic SPGs are fragile & break easily.

We will now look at setting up the regulators for the cylinders. The first thing you need to do is get the correct hose lengths. Let's start with the simple hoses, the high pressure hoses and the low pressure inflator hoses.

High pressure hoses

The most common length for the high pressure hoses is 6 inches/15 cm. That length seems to work well for most divers and positions the submersible pressure gauges (SPGs) in a good location so they are out of the way but still accessible. This length also works well for transmitters. The second most common length of high pressure hoses some people choose to use are 9 inches/ 22.5 cm. The 9 inch/22.5 cm long hoses (geezer hoses) help if you have to hold things a little farther from your eyes to be able to focus on them. In other words, if you're old enough to require reading glasses. The longer hoses work as long as the SPGs aren't hanging down too low and creating trenches in the bottom of the passage when you're moving through low swim-throughs. Most of the time they are stiff enough to not do this.

When choosing your SPGs, the options are plastic or brass SPGs. I recommend getting the brass ones. They are tougher and not as likely to break as the plastic ones. If you align the SPGs along the cylinders, they might snap back once you're done looking at them and possibly crack. The optimal size for sidemount is the smaller 1.5 inch/40 mm face SPGs. They are lighter and will not weigh the hose down. The 2 inch/50 mm face SPGs are also acceptable; however, you may notice the weight of the brass in those causes them to hang low in certain positions. This is especially true if you choose to use the small diameter braided high pressure hoses. When these SPGs are setup pointing up away from the cylinder and they hang down below the diver, I refer to them as curb feelers (we'll discuss this in chapter 9).

1.5 inch/40 mm & 2 inch/50 mm SPGs. The numbers are the same size making both easily readable.

Transmitters have grown in popularity over the past few years with more and more divers using them in place of SPGs. The main thing to remember with transmitters is to position them so that they are not at risk of breaking if you are moving through a swim through or wreck. Using HP hoses with transmitters helps maintain flexibility and allows you to secure them against the cylinders in a somewhat protected position.

Transmitters can be used in place of SPGs. If you are penetrating wrecks, make sure they are positioned in a well-protected location.

You need to decide where you want to position the SPGs. A very popular position for the SPGs is straight up from the 1st stage so the SPGs are located directly in front of the shoulders. This position makes it easy to view the faces of the SPGs; however, it could also cause them to hang low. This method works better with certain cylinder orientations or certain valve types. We'll discuss this more later in the book.

Another popular option is to route the SPGs alongside the cylinders rather than up in front of the shoulders. There are a couple of variations to this, but both keep the SPG up against the cylinder crown as seen in the photos here. This keeps the SPGs out of your way when you don't need them, yet allows them to be easily accessible when you want to see them.

Note the SPGs in front of both shoulders.

SPG positioned above and along the cylinder

You can have the SPG positioned along the cylinder above or below. Where it's positioned will depend on how you orient your valves. If the valves are facing up into your armpits, the SPGs will be above the cylinder. This may require a little more flexibility or you may need to pull the cylinder down a bit to view the face of the SPG. If the valves are facing down away from you, the SPGs will be below the cylinder. With this position, you just have to pull the SPG out to view it. One concern with the SPGs below the cylinder is their weight can allow them to hang a bit low.

A final option is to point the SPGs in toward the center of the chest so they are positioned in front of the chest. This keeps the SPGs out of the way, but does require the diver to pull them out to view. With everything going on in this area - dry suit inflator and wing inflator – positioning the SPGs across the chest creates a bit of a cluttered area.

Where you choose to position your SPGs shouldn't be a major issue. With only four options, you can try them all and see what works best for you. Just make sure they are accessible and streamlined and that you can read them easily.

1.5 inch/40 mm SPG on a 6 inch/15 cm hose routed down alongside cylinder

SPGs across the chest

SPG positioned below the cylinder on the left

Low pressure inflator hoses

Sidemount divers have used low pressure inflator hoses that measure anywhere in length from 8 inches/20 cm to 22 inches/55 cm and even longer. Any of these lengths work as long as the hoses are routed in such a way that they stay against the torso and streamlined, and they must not be so long that they stick out away from the diver. The length is going to be dependent on the port you choose, how you orient the 1st stages on your cylinders, and how you route the corrugated inflator hose.

Shorter hoses tend to be used when they are placed in the 5th port located on the end of some 1st stages. This allows the hoses to route directly across the chest to the low pressure inflator and dry suit inflator.

Longer hoses tend to be used when routing from a side port. While you can place the LP inflator hose in any port, it typically works best to use a port facing the cylinder body. With the hose positioned this way, it can be routed down toward your ribs and then back up under the shoulder strap and across to one of the inflators. This keeps the hoses streamlined and out of the way as well as reducing pressure on the 1st stage that can affect the position of the cylinder.

This is one issue with using the 5th port of the 1st stages. The cylinders

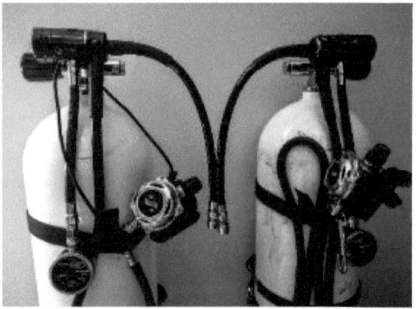

LP hoses coming off the 5th port. If these valves are positioned opening up without the valve being rotated, the LP hose can stick into your ribs causing discomfort. Valve down or rotating them avoids this.

LP hoses can be placed in a port facing the body of the cylinder (left) or away from the cylinder (right). Facing the cylinder allows for more streamlined hose routing.

LP hoses to inflator & dry suit. Both are in a port facing the cylinder & routed down then back up to the inflators.

With the valve opening to the rear and the handwheel positioned directly to the side, there is no room to place the LP hose in the 5th port. If using the 5th port of the 1st stage the valve must be rotated with the handwheel angled toward the back, otherwise there is no room for the LP hose without it sticking into your ribs.

must be clocked in such a way that the LP inflator hose is not rotating the cylinder out of trim. If you position the valve opening forward, the position is usually not affected because the 1st stages sit forward enough for the hoses to route straight across the chest. If you position the valve opening back, the handwheels should be angled slightly toward the back to avoid having the LP inflator hose poke into your ribs or cause your cylinders to rotate.

The one thing to be aware of when choosing low pressure inflator hose length is whether there is enough length for them to set evenly on the Schrader valve. Having too short of a hose can cause tension on it that will reduce the life of the o-ring inside. That o-ring is not easy to replace. When those start leaking, it's best to replace the hose. Another risk of having too short of a hose is breaking the power inflator. If you decide to play around and swing the cylinder forward to get through a narrow swim-through or wreck opening, the stress could be enough to break the inflator.

The final routing discussed is over the shoulder. Length of the low pressure inflator hose may need to be longer if you do not do the inflator/exhaust modification discussed in chapter 7. The length of the hose will have to be such that it can route up to the inflator and still allow for the hose to be raised to exhaust air from the wing. In this case, the optimal routing for the hose is around the back, over the shoulder, and down to the LP inflator.

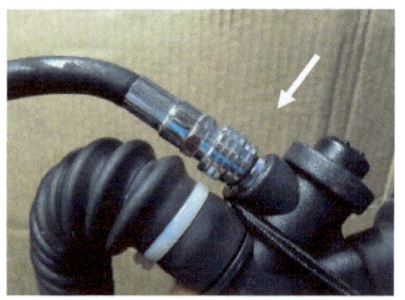

The gap at the top is slightly bigger than at the bottom causing wear on the o-ring & strain on the inflator.

One final topic of discussion is opposing valves. It is easy to ensure you have opposing valves on your own cylinders. However, there are likely to be times when you travel and all that's available are aluminum 80 cf/11 L cylinders with matching valves. If the dive center is agreeable, you can bring your own opposing valves and place them on the cylinders while there. The other option is to use the cylinders as they are.

In order to keep the handwheels easily accessible, you will have to orient the valves differently from each other. The left cylinder will have the valve opening back into your armpit, and the right cylinder will have the valve opening forward away from you. When this is necessary, I recommend positioning the SPGs alongside the cylinders to prevent the curb feeler effect on the right side. If you route your bungees around the cylinder necks, feed the right bungee between the cylinder neck and the hoses pointing down toward the cylinder body, not over the hoses as this will affect the cylinder trim. Other than those minor changes, the cylinders will dive just like cylinders with opposing valves. The key is to be flexible. Don't let the lack of opposing valves affect

Inflator hose routed over shoulder

your trip. Sidemount gear set up is about improvising to make it work. This is especially true when options are limited.

C-53 Wreck, Cozumel, Mexico

5 SETTING UP 2ND STAGE REGULATORS

Let's move on to a discussion about regulator hoses and 2nd stage regulators. I saved this discussion for last and made it into its own chapter because there are many more options available. Take your time reading this and weigh the advantages and disadvantages of each option.

Traditional backmount hoses – one long, one short

Backmount style hose setup – Long hose on one 1st stage and short hose on the other 1st stage. Each 1st stage also has an LP inflator hose. The only difference from backmount besides hose lengths is the addition of a second SPG.

Probably the most common hose routing in sidemount is the traditional backmount routing. It's simple and well established. The regulator hose coming from the left cylinder is the shorter of the two, routed around the neck and held in place by a necklace bungee. The long hose comes from the right cylinder and is routed across the torso, around the neck, and clipped to a chest D-ring when not in use. The excess length of the right hose is secured onto the right cylinder using hose retainers.

If you happen to already be using a backmounted twinset, all you need to purchase are an LP inflator hose, regulator hose, two short HP hoses, and an SPG. With this routing method, the left regulator hose length will again depend on cylinder position and body type, but the most common lengths are 32 inches/80 cm if used without a swivel and 31 inches/77 cm if used with a swivel (more on this shortly). The right hose can be 5 feet/150 cm or 7 feet/210 cm long. Either length will do for recreational diving.

If you are transitioning from a single cylinder to sidemount diving, you should consider a complete new regulator set unless you are already starting with a good regulator and don't plan on diving single cylinder backmount again. If you do the latter, you will need matching 1ˢᵗ stages and a 2ⁿᵈ stage regulator that is as good as your primary regulator. An octo won't do because you'll be breathing from it during half of the dive. You will also want to consider using DIN 1ˢᵗ stages rather than yoke.

There has been a lot of discussion about whether there is even a need for a long hose in sidemount configuration. One argument is that with two independent cylinders the likelihood of losing all air in both cylinders is very small. While this is true, the loss of the use of one cylinder is a possibility. And while proper air management should negate the need for any more air than what's left in the working cylinder, increased air consumption can create a need to share air with a team member if a long swim back to the entry point is necessary. There's also the possibility of diving mixed teams. You shouldn't limit yourself to diving only with other sidemount divers. And when diving with single cylinder divers, a longer hose can be useful. Let's now discuss variations from the traditional backmount routing.

Long hose tucked into hose retainers on cylinder

One long, one short variations

The first variation is swapping which cylinders the long and short hoses are connected to – the long hose to the left cylinder and the short hose to the right cylinder. The reasoning behind this method is to keep the long hose from crossing the torso. If you use a corded canister primary light, this can prevent the long hose from getting trapped under the light cord (dependent on where you mount the canister and with which hand you hold the light). You don't want to trap the long hose in the event of having to share air. When you deploy the long hose in an air sharing event, you should deploy the entire length of it. This is especially important if you have to conduct your safety stop while staggered along an anchor line. If the hose is routed across the chest and trapped under a light cord, that will prevent it from being able to fully deploy. You won't get the advantage of the full length of the hose.

44

Smaller reversible 2nd stage regulator with the exhaust to the side allowing it to be positioned with the hose coming from either side.

You can also choose variations based on whether the hose routes around your neck or directly to your mouth. With the long hose on the left cylinder, it's easier to route the short hose from the right cylinder directly to your mouth without going around your neck. The one thing to keep in mind with this is the type of 2nd stage regulators you use. The most common 2nd stage regulator is somewhat heavy and can cause jaw fatigue early during a dive. There are mouthpieces that help reduce the jaw fatigue, but you still have the weight of the 2nd stage on your mouth. There are smaller, lightweight 2nd stage regulators you can purchase to deal with this. If you choose to use your standard 2nd stage regulator, by routing the hose around your neck, a good portion of the weight of the regulator is on the neck rather than your jaw.

Another consideration is if you route the hose from the left cylinder directly to your mouth, a reversible 2nd stage will be necessary unless you are okay with the hose crossing your chest. A reversible 2nd stage is one which allows you to have the hose come off either side or can be used in a position that would be considered upside down. If you try to use a standard 2nd stage regulator with the hose routed directly to your mouth, the hose will stick out a bit more from your chest.

Standard 2nd stage regulator with short hose routed directly to mouth. Notice how the hose is forced into an awkward position.

Two short hoses – direct to mouth

One of the original routings used by sidemount divers was having the regulator hoses come directly to their mouths without routing around the neck. This is still in use by some sidemount divers. One advantage of this is it minimizes the setup by allowing for the use of shorter hoses that route directly to the mouth. The hoses do not cross the chest, so there is less clutter in front of the diver. Typically, this requires a regulator with the exhaust to the side that can be used in either orientation or a reversible 2nd stage coming off the left side cylinder. While it's not absolutely necessary as you can use a slightly longer hose and route it across your chest (just discussed), it defeats the original purpose of this method. Also, as previously mentioned, smaller 2nd stages work better to prevent jaw fatigue.

The hose length will vary depending on how the cylinders are carried, the body of the diver, and whether swivels on the 2nd stages are used. The easiest way to determine proper hose length is to take a hose that you know is too long, get in the water with the rig properly trimmed, and mark the location on the hose where it meets the corner of your mouth with your head turned toward the opposite direction from the cylinder the hose is attached to. Most hoses have white lettering along their lengths, so noting what word or letter is sufficient to provide a close enough idea of the necessary length. Do not attempt to determine the hose length out of the water. The cylinders set differently while standing up on land than they do when in proper trim in the water.

There are a couple of disadvantages with using shorter hoses routed directly to the mouth. The first is air sharing becomes a difficult task. With a short hose, you and your buddy will have to be very close to each other to share air. This won't be a problem in open water where you can get into a vertical orientation and ascend facing each other. You will be in close quarters, though. Using short hoses also eliminates the possibility of diving in mixed teams (with single cylinder divers) unless everyone is agreeable to treating it as a solo dive among friends.

The second issue is that the regulator hoses could stick out when the regulator is not in use. With this configuration, common hose length will be somewhere in the 12 inch/30 cm long range. With the chest D-rings in the most common location directly over the pectoralis (chest) muscle, pulling a regulator from your mouth and clipping it onto the D-ring will cause the hose to bend out. This can be addressed by relocating the D-ring from the chest to a location higher on the shoulder where the hose remains stretched to its full length. Or you can simply add D-rings to your shoulder straps positioned to the side of your neck where the hose will remain stretched when not in use.

Regulator hose bends out if not properly routed.

None of this means this routing is a bad idea. Just be aware of the potential issues so you can address and avoid them. And have a plan for air sharing in the rare instance that it may be necessary.

Two short hoses – around the neck

Another option is to use slightly longer regulator hoses and route them both around the neck. This eliminates the need for smaller, lighter, reversible 2nd stages. The hose on the right cylinder will need to be slightly longer than the hose on the left cylinder (typically 40 inches/100 cm), but both are routed around the neck so the weight of the 2nd stage is partially supported. With this method, you can either secure one 2nd stage to a necklace bungee around the neck (typically the one from the left cylinder) and secure the other one with a bolt snap to your right side chest D-ring when not in use. Or you can use a double regulator bungee necklace to secure both 2nd stages.

With this routing method, air sharing becomes a little easier. The longer hose coming off of the right side cylinder has enough length to allow a little more space between divers, so you won't have to be so close to each other as you ascend to the surface. You will also need to make sure the shorter hose coming off of the left cylinder is placed around your neck before you place the longer hose from the right cylinder around your neck. This will keep the longer hose from being trapped under the shorter hose. When you get in the water and don your gear, before beginning the dive remove the 2nd stage you intend to donate from around your neck and hold it out in front of you. If it's trapped, it will be held back by the other 2nd stage hose.

Two long hoses

The final method uses two long hoses. Some divers choose to use a long hose on each side because they want to be able to donate whichever 2nd stage they are breathing from without thinking about it. This is acceptable, but you will need to carefully evaluate the possible hose routings while setting this up. As with any of the other methods discussed, you can route the hoses as you like as long as you're aware of the issues they might create. The easiest routing is directly to the mouth as this will prevent the trapping of either hose by the other. You'll have to use a reversible 2nd stage on the left side or run the hose across your chest, keeping in mind what was mentioned in a previous chapter.

Another option is to route the left hose around the neck. This makes it mandatory that the right hose is routed directly to the mouth. If you route both long hoses around your neck, one will always be trapped under the other unless you reroute the hoses with every regulator switch. While this may seem like a minor inconvenience, it's not practical to do while diving and the chance of not routing them correctly is greater.

The best option is to route both hoses directly to the mouth so your muscle memory for regulator donation is the same regardless of which 2nd stage you are breathing from. If you route one hose around the neck, then you still have to remember whether you can grab the hose and hold the 2nd stage out for your buddy or you need to pull the hose from around your neck in order to deploy it and donate the 2nd stage. This defeats the purpose of using two long hoses. You'll still have to think about which regulator you are breathing from. Some will argue that it also allows you to choose which cylinder you are donating from but, again, you'll have to make a decision during a split second of seeing the out of air signal. And you really should manage your air so that it doesn't matter which 2nd stage you donate (more on that later).

Securing your 2nd stage

When you're not breathing from a 2nd stage regulator, it has to be secured somewhere. You have a few options available for doing this. If it's not a regulator you will be donating in an out of air situation, you can secure it around your neck in a necklace bungee in the traditional manner with the bungee secured to the 2nd stage, or you can secure it using a standard bolt snap. If it is a 2nd stage you will be donating during an out of air situation, you need to be able to do so quickly. Taking the time to try to open a bolt snap and unclip it from a D-ring isn't acceptable, especially if you wear thick gloves.

Traditionally, divers have secured bolt snaps to regulators using #24 cave line. This is somewhat permanent and requires the diver to unclip the regulator to donate it. The time it may take to do this can be the difference between life and death.

In sidemount configuration, it is necessary to have a breakaway system in place to hold the bolt snap to the regulator hose because you may not be donating the 2nd stage you are breathing in an out of air situation. If a diver signals out of air, there won't be time to wait for you to fumble with a bolt snap. It's unlikely that the diver knew about the out of air at the end of a full breath from the regulator. Even with regular practice, unclipping the regulator will take longer than breaking it away.

The most common way to set up a breakaway system is with a zip tie or o-ring. If you use a zip tie, make sure it is a smaller one and you can easily break it. You should be able to break it by simply exerting some force on it as you pull the 2nd stage away from the D-ring. If this does not break it, a slight twist in the 2nd stage will increase the force on the zip tie.

Zip tie holding bolt snap on swivel

Zip ties stashed in the pocket in the back of a set of wetnotes

Bungee loop breakaway

You need to practice donating your 2nd stage regularly by breaking the zip tie as you deploy the 2nd stage from the clipped position. Practicing to release the bolt snap builds that into muscle memory and when the situation arises in a true time of need, that is what you will revert to. So pull the 2nd stage away from the D-ring and push it forward as if donating it. If the hose is routed around the neck, pull the hose over the head as well. The only way to build muscle memory is to practice repetitively.

Once you've done that, retrieve the broken zip tie and replace it with a new one. The bolt snap will be attached to the D-ring. I carry a small bag of zip ties in my pocket for this very reason. The broken zip tie goes into the bag and a new one is pulled out.

You can also use a bungee loop that goes around the mouthpiece and has a bolt snap secured to it and is clipped onto your chest D-ring. There are even systems available by manufacturers that will allow for a breakaway. One such system is a small Delrin or plastic clip to which the regulator hose can be snapped into and out of. Another is a magnet system. One magnet is attached to your chest D-ring and the other is attached to your 2nd stage regulator. When not in use, the magnets are strong enough to hold the 2nd stage in place but break away easily with force is applied.

Necklace bungees are another method used to secure the 2nd stage regulators. Some divers use a bungee on one regulator and a bolt snap on the other. Some also use a necklace bungee with a breakaway support for both regulators. This method holds the regulators in a location where they can be easily accessed, breathed from, and allow for quick deployment if necessary. Just be careful because that bungee may snap back at you after it's stretched!

Some divers also use a double ender secured to the 2nd stage regulator with bungee. The double ender is clipped onto a D-ring when the regulator is not in use. The 2nd stage can be pulled out of the bungee quickly if needed, leaving the double ender clipped to the D-ring. The disadvantage of this method is that you are adding the weight of the double ender to your 2nd stage and this can contribute to jaw fatigue. It is also more difficult to deploy the 2nd stage because the bungee has to go over the face of the 2nd stage rather than over the mouthpiece.

Swivels and 2nd stages

The final topic of discussion dealing with regulator hoses is the use of swivels on 2nd stage regulators. There are two different types of swivels available for use by divers - the 360 swivels and the fixed angle swivels. The fixed angle swivels are available in a 90 degree and 110 degree option and seem to be more common. The reason for this is that they have

Delrin breakaway

Magnetic breakaway – the hose feeds through the hole and the other end is attached to a D-ring.

Double regulator bungee necklace

Double ender bungee breakaway

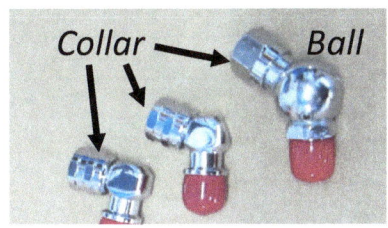

First two swivels are the 90 & 110 degree fixed. The only moving part and location of the o-ring is the collar.
Far right is a 360 degree swivel. In addition to having a collar like the fixed swivels, the 360 swivel also rotates around the ball and has an o-ring inside the ball.

less failure points than the 360 swivels and require less maintenance.

The fixed swivel has one moving part and one o-ring. The only moving part is the collar that screws onto the 2nd stage regulator. In addition to that same moving part and o-ring, the 360 swivel has an o-ring in the ball, and that part of the swivel also rotates. A common issue with these is the screw holding the two halves of the ball joint together comes loose and it begins to leak. Making sure the screw is snug and there are no bubbles escaping from it before every dive helps prevent this from happening, however, that is an additional failure point not present on the fixed swivel. I have even seen ball joints come completely apart. There are instructors that will not allow their students to use these under any circumstances.

The advantage to using a swivel is that you get a much tighter hose routing regardless of whether you route the hoses around your neck or directly to your mouth. This also helps reduce jaw fatigue even more. With no swivel, the hose bows out and puts more tension on the 2nd stage regulator.

The disadvantage is that swivels can take getting used to. When donating a regulator with a swivel in an out of air emergency, you need to make sure the swivel is in the proper orientation so as not to make

The hose is closer to the head & the 2nd stage is centered on the left where a swivel is used. Compare to the hose & off center 2nd stage on the right with no swivel.

the 2nd stage uncomfortable for the air recipient. This is a little easier with a fixed swivel because it only rotates one way.

Setting up your regulators

Choosing the appropriate port for each hose is important. This will depend on which hose routing you choose and the location of the ports on your 1st stages. Here are some general guidelines to follow.

1. Screw your 1st stages onto your cylinders so you have a visual of how they will look. The prime consideration is leaving the valve handwheels clear to access during an emergency closure.

The 1st stage on the left cylinder left leaves the handwheel accessible. The 1st stage on the right blocks it making valve closure difficult.

2. You need to decide how you want to position your 1st stages. Whether they are in toward you or out away from you will determine which direction you can point your SPGs. Standard valves can go in any direction. There's one thing to consider if you position your 1st stages in toward you. In that orientation, the SPGs may be more difficult to reach and require greater flexibility when they are positioned alongside the cylinders because they will be above the cylinders and behind you.

Angled valve. Note the angle of the HP hose and SPG.

3. If you have angled valves on your cylinders, this will limit your options. With angled valves, the optimal orientation is to face the valves forward away from you because of where this positions the HP ports. Facing them away allows you to position the SPGs either up into your shoulders or in toward your chest. Any other position places the SPGs out too far from your body and cylinders due to the angle.

The long hose must screw into a port positioned down toward the cylinder allowing the hose to be streamlined and secured to the cylinder by hose retainers.

4.   Once you've determined the orientation of the valves, screw the high pressure hoses and SPGs into the 1st stages.

5.   If you are using short regulator hoses, you will want to put them into ports that are pointing up toward you. You don't want to create a loop in the hoses by having them routed down toward the cylinder and then looped back up to your mouth.

6.   If you are using a long hose, you will need to screw it into a port that points down toward the cylinder. This will allow it to be easily secured by hose retainers onto the body of the cylinder.

7.   Low pressure inflator hoses can come out of the 1st stage from pretty much any position discussed. Routing will depend on your sidemount rig and the length of the hoses. Although positioning them in a 5th port or down provides the lowest profile.

You may find that you will need to try a few different variations with your hose routing until you find the one that works best for your regulators. I've offered you several options in this chapter. You might have already eliminated some of them based on what you've read. Don't be afraid to try a few different options if the first one doesn't quite work for you.

SPG pointing up, down alongside cylinder, and across chest.

6 CUSTOMIZING YOUR SIDEMOUNT RIG
BUNGEE MODIFICATIONS

Because there are different reasons for sidemount diving and because manufacturers try to meet general market demand, you are likely to want to customize your rig soon after you make your purchase. There isn't a sidemount system that will be ready to dive out of the bag without any adjustments or modifications. At least not if you want it to be low profile and streamlined. It may be as simple as a minor modification, like the bungees you use to hold the cylinders in position, or a major modification, like changing the routing of the shoulder straps to the waist straps. Whatever modifications you make, you'll find that when you customize your rig to fit your body type and your diving style, you will feel much better when diving in sidemount.

There's a lot to be said about bungees and their function in sidemount, so this entire chapter is dedicated to discussing that one aspect of sidemount rigs. Bungees can serve a couple of purposes on a sidemount rig. The main function, and the most important one, is to hold the valves of the cylinders in the armpits so the cylinders are trimmed out on a horizontal plane with the body. While in many cases the bottoms of the cylinders hang off of rails or D-rings on the rear of the sidemount rig, you can't do that with the valves as it would be impossible to clip them onto a D-ring located behind you near your shoulder blades. At least most of us are not quite that flexible!

As mentioned in chapter 3, the original method used to pull the cylinder valves into the armpits was bicycle innertube routed around the back. As sidemount has evolved and manufacturers began producing rigs specifically for sidemount, the manner in which we pull the valves up has also evolved. The first manufactured system used bungee with a bolt snap and quick link.

Some sidemount systems come with standard 3/8 inch/94 mm bungee cut to a certain length (anywhere from 13 inches/32.5 cm to 19 inches/47.5 cm) with a quick link on one end and a stainless steel bolt snap on the other. The quick link is attached to a 1 inch/2.5 cm D-ring on the back of the harness, routed under the arm, and the bolt snap is clipped to one of the chest D-rings (usually the bottom D-ring if two D-rings are present). While this system does keep the cylinder valve from hanging freely under the diver, it typically doesn't pull the cylinder up far enough into the armpit.

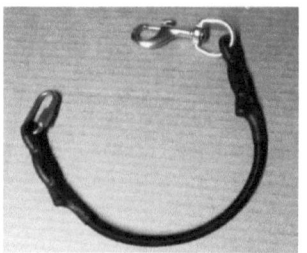

Original commercial sidemount bungee with quick link attached to rear & bolt snap attached to chest

Because the bolt snap on the front end tends to stick straight out from the D-ring, it doesn't allow the neck of the cylinder to be pulled up completely. It actually pushes the cylinder forward and causes it to ride too low in front of the diver's body. This bungee system can also pull the cylinders inward tight to your body. While at first that might sound like a desirable feature, it can push the cylinders into the diver's ribs and be uncomfortable. Ideally, you want a bungee system that pulls the valves up into the armpits, not in toward the torso.

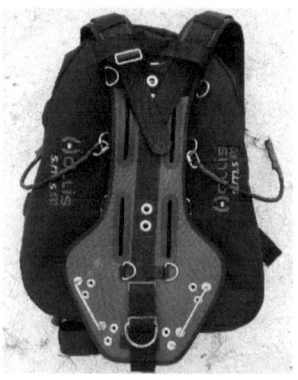

Original routing of bungees over the top of the wing to allow for air entrapment

If you choose to stay with this bungee system, there are a couple of ways you can route the bungee from the back to the front. The original design of this system is for the bungees to route over the top of horseshoe or donut shaped wings. The purpose of this is to trap air in the lower portion of the wing to allow greater lift lower on the body. Remember reading in chapter 2 that sidemount rigs are designed to put most of the lift lower on the back. That's the idea in trapping some of the air in the lower portion

Bolt snap on bungee prevents the valve from being pulled up into the armpit

Bungee squeezing wing can cause air to be trapped.

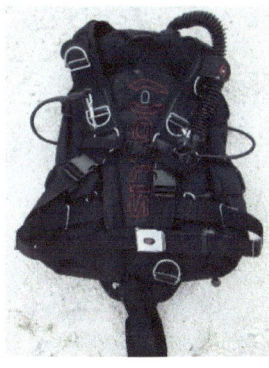

Standard routing of original bungees

Wing without the bungee routed over it. Note the height of the wing.

of the wing. This system effectively traps air in the lower portion of the wing by creating a restriction in the upper portion and putting more of the lift at the bottom. The trapping of air is part of the design of this system, but it can also be an issue making it difficult to purge air from the wing when needed. An even bigger problem exists, which we'll discuss in detail in chapter 9.

A simple modification to this bungee routing is to route the bungee beneath the wing rather than over it. This routing keeps air from being trapped at the bottom of the wing. That does mean less lift toward the feet, which we'll address later. It also allows the edges of the wing to curl up like a taco shell. Manufacturers have tried to address this with bungee inside the wing used to pull the edges in. It isn't enough, as only the inside of the wing that sits against your back gets pulled in. Air is still pushing the exposed side up creating a larger profile in the water, which is less streamlined and creates drag.

We need to prevent the wing from doing this. Alternative methods can be used to achieve a flatter wing. The idea is to keep the wing flat against the back while also keeping air from being trapped in it. Because the objective is to keep the wing as flat and low profile as possible, most are already made with tabs or grommets to help do this. These rigs come with the bungee just described that is positioned against your back with the intent being to hold the edges of the wing down. However, because this bungee is attached to the middle part of the wing, it only pulls the edges in, not down, so it isn't very effective. The edges of the wing need to be secured to the front of your torso to get the most streamlined rig possible.

A method that works well is to attach the wing to the bungees from underneath. You can either route the bungees through a tab or grommet that's already located on the wing or, with some of the older wings, you may have to burn a hole into the tab that guides the bungee under the wing or have a tab sewn onto the wing. Since I first published this method on my website years ago, some manufacturers have modified their wings to include a tab for this purpose.

Bungee routing under wing to prevent air entrapment. Note the smaller bungee routed along the inside of the wing.

Another bungee system that is used by some divers is the ring system. The ring bungee system is designed to pull the cylinder valves up into the armpits close to the body. Ring bungees are designed to be used with a choker system. The choker is wrapped around the neck of the cylinder and holds the bolt snap against the valve. Ring bungees can pull the cylinder valves up close enough, but their design makes it difficult to do this. In order to work well, the ring bungees must be short enough to pull the cylinders into the armpits. This means when they are not in use and the bungee is relaxed, the rings end up resting near the backs of the arms. In order to reach them and pull them forward, you need to be very flexible. While this might be achievable with the first cylinder attached to the ring, the second one is usually much more difficult because the first one is already putting tension on the rig. What usually happens is that divers who use the ring bungee system position the rings too far forward during setup so they can be reached. The longer bungee doesn't pull the valves up as far as they should be, so they ride too low in front of the diver rather than at the sides.

Bungee attachment under wing through a tab already sewn onto the edge. Because the other end of the bungee is secured to the front of the harness, this stretches the wing laterally & pulls it against the diver's back.

A third bungee method used, and possibly the most common over the last several years, is

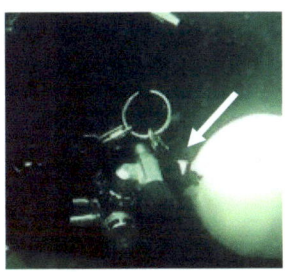

Choker used to hold the bolt snap against the neck of the cylinder

Ring bungee in use. These rings are positioned properly, so they pull the valves up to the location where they need to be.

the loop bungee. As mentioned previously, the loop bungee was one of the original methods used when sidemount first came to North Florida. Some divers used bicycle inner tubes wrapped around their backs and looped over the cylinder valves. This has evolved into the use of bungee, but the concept is the same.

The advantage to the loop bungee system is that the loops pull the cylinders up into the armpits to the position where they should be. These bungees do not pull the valves into the body and do not have any hardware that pushes the cylinders out from the rig. There are a variety of ways to set up a loop bungee system on your rig. They differ in how they are secured to the back of the rig and how the loop is used over the valve.

One of the common methods of routing the loop bungee when used with a horseshoe wing is to run the end of the bungee through a piece of 2 inch/5 cm webbing that is routed through the back of the harness. The webbing can be placed on the inside or the outside of the harness and wing. The difference will be whether you are trying to impede the flow of air from the bottom of the wing to the top or not. The 2 inch/5 cm webbing does create less

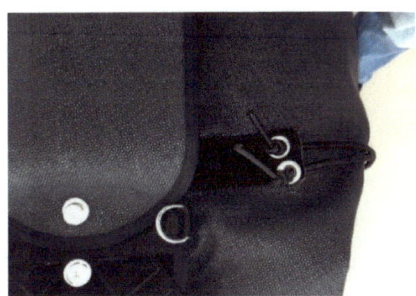

Bungee attached using 2 inch/5 cm webbing. Left shows the webbing on top of the wing. Right shows the webbing under the wing. Note this bungee also routes through a tab at the edge.

air entrapment because the pressure on the wing is spread out over a wider area than with bungee alone. With this system, it helps to attach the webbing to the harness with a sex bolt or triglide so it cannot slide back and forth and affect the position of the loops.

Another loop bungee method is to create a loop with bungee and run it through an attachment point on the back of the harness. This can be done on one of the 1 inch/2.5 cm D-rings present on some harnesses. If your harness doesn't have any hardware on the top rear, you can still secure the bungee using a triglide over the spine webbing. Triglides with holes laterally positioned have even been developed specifically for securing the bungee to the spine webbing. You can use two pieces of bungee, one for each side, or a single, continuous piece. If you use a single piece, it's advisable to place knots around the attachment point on the spine to restrict it from sliding back and forth and causing the cylinder valves to hang unevenly.

If you are using a rig with a smaller pillow shaped wing, you might be able route the bungee through the grommets positioned at the edge of the wing. As previously mentioned, some pillow shaped wings come with grommets along the edges of the wing to be used with belly bands to keep the wing flat against your back. If the wing is tall enough, the grommets near the top of the wing can be used to route the loop bungees through. You will need to place a knot on the inside of the wing so that when the loop bungee

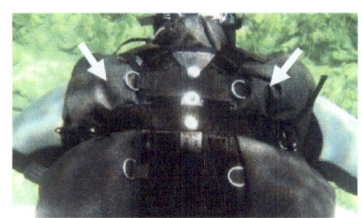

Bungee attached using 2 inch/5 cm webbing over the top of the wing

Single length of bungee held in place on spine webbing with triglide.

Triglide with bungee loop holes

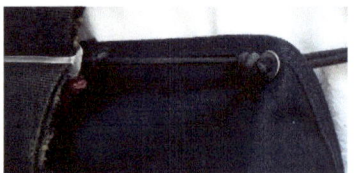

Loop bungee routed through grommet on wing with a knot to the inside to pull the wing flat across the back. There is also a knot next to the triglide to prevent the bungee from sliding.

Bungee stretches the wing across the back to maintain a low profile even when partially inflated.

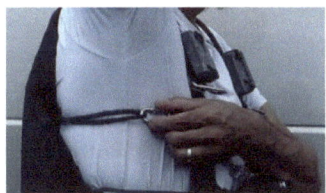

Proper position of loop bungee under arm. With a dry suit or wetsuit on, the end of the loop will be right at the seam.

The bungee gets pulled around the cylinder valve.

is pulled, it stretches the wing across your back. The bungee can be routed over or under the wing, depending on your preference.

The length of the loop bungees should be about midway between your chest and your back when they are relaxed without the cylinders in them. The exact length will be dependent on whether you face your valves forward or backward and how you secure the valves in the loops, but variation should be an inch/couple of centimeters or so at most. Just cut the bungee a little long because you can always shorten it, but lengthening it can be problematic.

To secure the loop over the valve, the bungee will need to go over the handwheel without hindering your ability to open and close the valve. The most common routing of the bungee is to simply pull it over the outside of the handwheel. The small lip created by the handwheel over the brass will prevent the bungee from easily slipping off. There is also a slight rotation in the cylinder because of where the lower clip is positioned along the cylinder. That helps keep the bungee in place as well.

There is a disadvantage to this routing of the bungee. As mentioned, there is a slight cylinder rotation. This works to keep the cylinder in its proper place tucked into the armpit and parallel to the body. However, as some cylinders get breathed and become lighter, they begin to rotate too much due to the pull from the bungee. The bungee pulls the valve handwheel up more while the bottom of the cylinder hangs from the lower leash in a fixed position. There isn't enough weight on the bottom of the cylinder to counteract this rotation and keep it in place, so the cylinder rotates around that fixed lower attachment throwing it out of trim.

This does not happen with every type of cylinder. Galvanized and concave bottom steel cylinders typically have enough weight at the bottom of the cylinder that they will not rotate. The design of these cylinders places enough weight at the bottom that they remain negatively buoyant even when they are nearly empty. Painted steel cylinders will behave differently depending on size and type. The longer the cylinder, the more likely you are to have rotation sooner during the dive. Shorter cylinders, such as an LP 95 cf/15 L cylinder, can be breathed down significantly more before they begin to rotate. Aluminum 80 cf/11 L cylinders will begin rotation almost immediately. I don't recommend this method be used with these cylinders at all.

An alternative method you can use to secure the valves to the bungees and use the rotation to your advantage is to route the bungee inside the valve, in between the valve and your ribs, pull the bungee around the front of the valve, and then up over the handwheel. This puts the rotational tension of the bungee downward from the handwheel rather than straight up. The handwheel rotates down and in toward the body rather than up and out away from the body. The bungee loop will need to be slightly longer to get it over the handwheel with this routing, but it will keep the cylinders from rotating up. This is only necessary with the lighter, painted steel cylinders and aluminum cylinders.

The loop then gets placed over the handwheel.

Once in front of the handwheel, release it so it sits inside the lip of the handwheel.

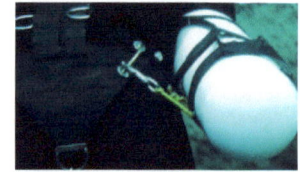

Cylinder rotating on lower attachment point when it's about half full.

A final method, one which I prefer using with aluminum 80 cf/11 L cylinders, is a slightly modified version of the loop. Rather than pull the loop over the handwheel and create any kind of rotational tension on the cylinder, I prefer to route the bungee around the neck. With this method, you must have a small bolt snap attached to the loop bungee. The bungee is routed around the neck and clipped onto a chest D-ring. The reason for a small bolt snap is to prevent the valve from being pushed forward by the bolt snap. This method only works with lighter aluminum cylinders because it pulls the cylinder into your body rather than up into your armpit. The cylinders need to be light enough to allow the bungee to pull them up and into the armpit. This isn't possible with steel cylinders.

Regardless of what method you use, you might want to attach the bungee to the front of the rig so it is easily accessible once you put it on. It does no good for you to put your rig on and have the bungee stuck between your rig and your back. Securing the bungee to the front can be done quite easily with a quick link and small bolt snap or some static cord. The bungee just needs to be attached to one of the D-rings on the front of the rig or to the harness webbing directly. The only purpose of this attachment is to make it easier to grab the bungee when donning your cylinders. The hardware/cord is not intended to be used to hold the cylinders up and should just hang freely next to your valve once the bungee is secured around the handwheel.

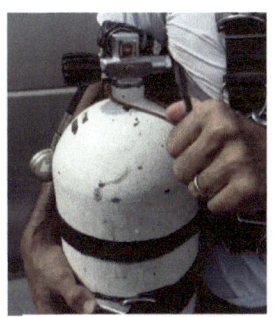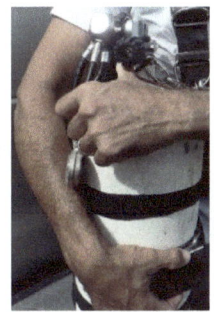

Inside rotation method. From top left to right, then bottom - The bungee is pulled past the valve on the opposite side of the handwheel. If there is a post on that side you can either place the post inside the loop or route the bungee under it. Pull the bungee across the valve & over the handwheel. This places the rotational force of the bungee pulling the handwheel down so the cylinder does not rotate up on the lower attachment.

No matter what method you choose to use, make sure you experiment with various thicknesses of bungee. Most rigs come with thicker 3/8 inch/94 mm bungee. While this works well, the thicker bungee is more difficult to stretch forward to put around the valve, and if routed around the handwheel can easily pop off because the lip created by the handwheel isn't significant enough to hold it. Thinner 3/16 inch/48 mm bungee works just as well and holds up just as long. It has the same strength rating yet is not as difficult to stretch to get over the handwheel. I used the same 3/16 inch/48 mm bungee that I had on my Florida sidemount rig for more than 10 years and almost 2000 dives before I finally had to replace it! Most of my dives were in freshwater and the rig always got a nice long freshwater rinse dive after being in salt water, so length of usability may vary. Bungee is inexpensive, though.

As you can see, there are a few options when it comes to the bungee system on your sidemount rig. Try them and see what works best for you and the configuration you are diving. There isn't a single method that is superior to the others. I personally use three different methods regularly depending on what rig and cylinders I'm using.

Static line holding bungee in place

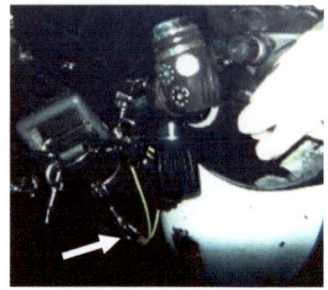

Note the static line hanging freely. The cylinder is held up by the bungee loop. The static line serves no purpose when in the water.

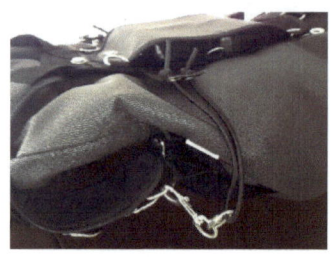

Bolt snap and quick link holding bungee in place

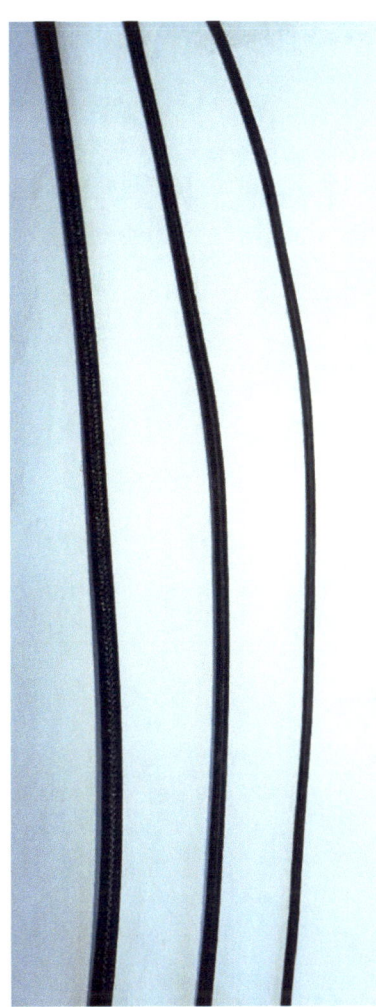

Variety of bungee widths. Bottom is 3/8 inch/94 mm bungee. Top is 3/16 inch/48 mm bungee. The thinner bungee is just as durable as the thicker bungee but less difficult to pull and place around the valve. It's also more likely to remain held in place by the handwheel.

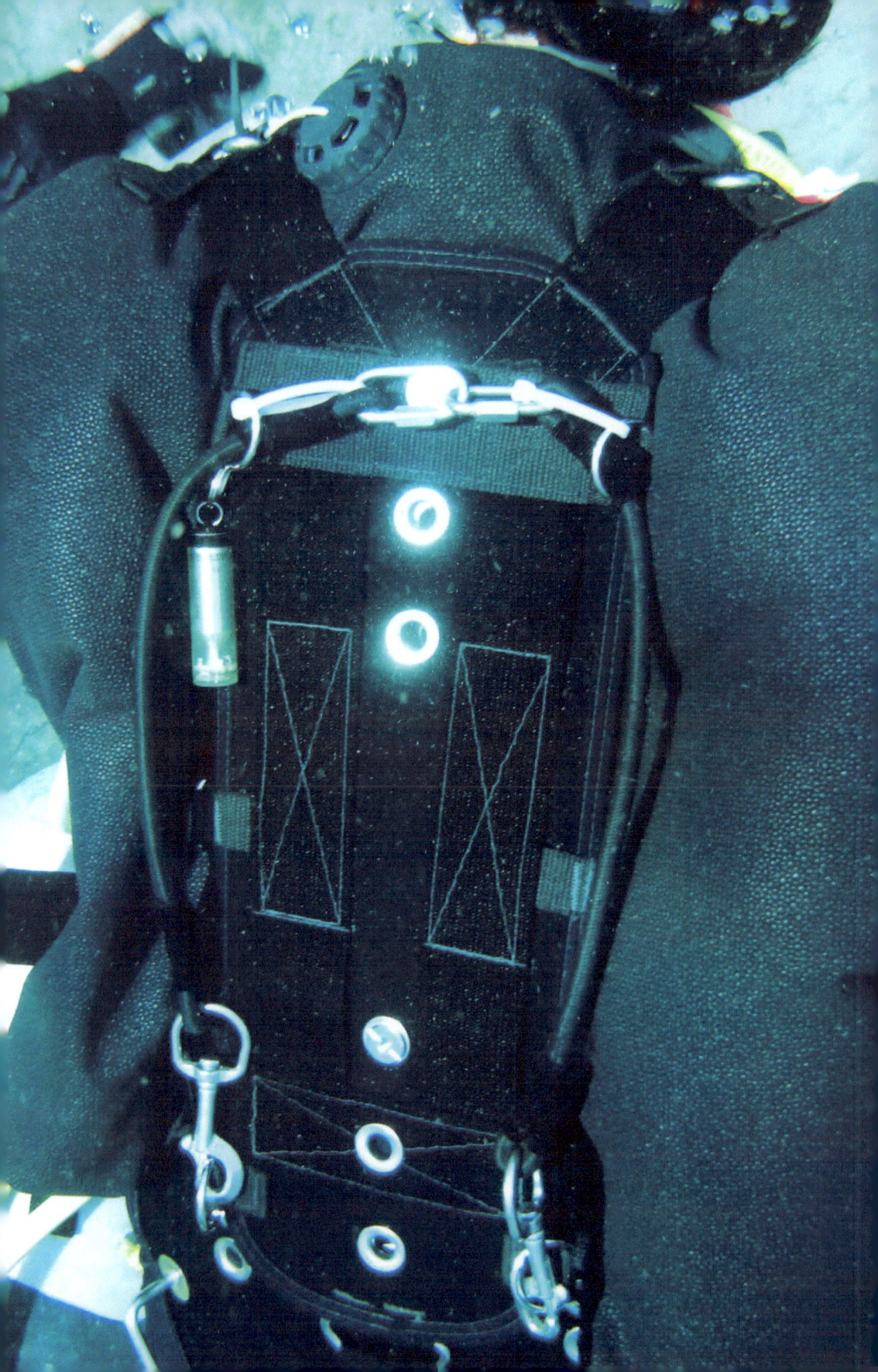

7 CUSTOMIZING YOUR SIDEMOUNT RIG
WING MODIFICATIONS

We spent an entire chapter discussing the bungees on a sidemount rig. They play an integral role in keeping our cylinders properly trimmed, so they deserve a lot of time in this book and on your part to make sure they work properly for you. There are other aspects of the sidemount rig that are also important that we'll cover in this chapter.

Inflator/exhaust modifications

Horseshoe and Donut Shaped Wings

A common modification that can be made to rigs with horseshoe or donut shaped wings involves the inflator and exhaust ports. The first manufactured sidemount rig came with the inflator on the shoulder and the exhaust on the inside bottom of the wing. These are the traditional positions used on wings and BCDs. While this may work for backmount for a variety of reasons, it's not optimal in sidemount.

In order to exhaust air from the wing, you need to get the area you are expelling the air from higher than the rest of the wing. With an exhaust port at the hip, this means getting your feet slightly higher than your head. When expelling air from the inflator, you not only need to get your shoulders slightly higher than the rest of the wing, but you also must raise the corrugated hose above the port on the wing. In backmount, with a cylinder on your back, all you have to do is get into a feet up or head up position to allow the air to rise out of the wing. You don't need to get completely vertical. You just need to get that part of the wing higher than the rest of it. In backmount, all aspects of the wing are also not stretched laterally and pulled down completely so the hip of the wing where the exhaust is located on the inside is able to roll up to get to the highest point. This isn't the case in sidemount. When properly streamlined, the wing is held against your back. You also can't get the exhaust to the highest point unless it's located on the outside of the wing. Having the corrugated inflator hose coming off the hip and the exhaust port located on the top of the shoulder works best because it's already at the highest point. All you have to do is pull the exhaust port open to release air. This probably wasn't the reason this exchange was originally done, though.

Swapping the exhaust to the top was likely initially done for the purpose of protecting the inflator hose elbow in overhead environments. With traditional backmount wings, the elbow is protected by the cylinder on the back. With the cylinders moved away from the back to the sides, the elbow is exposed. Swapping the two resulted in placing the elbow in a protected location under the wing near the hip. If you look closely at the elbow on your wing, you'll notice the seam, which is its weakest area, runs down the center of the outer side. It doesn't take much force to break this seam, especially when it smacks against something hard like the inside of a wreck or a dive boat in rough conditions.

Exposed elbow on shoulder

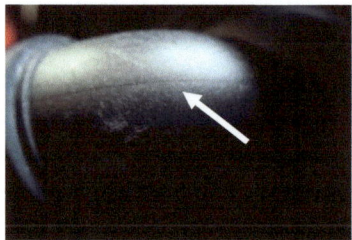

Note the seam of the elbow

If you're not planning on diving inside of a wreck or when conditions are rough enough to toss a dive boat around, is it necessary? Swapping the elbow and exhaust positions the exhaust in a location that allows for easier release of air from a horizontal position. With the exhaust over the left shoulder, it is a matter of pulling the dump cord to open the exhaust valve and allow air to rise out of the wing. You never have to break trim. This modification is simple to make. Before doing this, you must have the rig properly sized for you. The exhaust valve cord needs to be the right length for you to reach without hanging too low or being too short that it gets pulled open when you're in the water.

First, unscrew the exhaust valve and the inflator hose from their original locations. Screw the inflator valve onto the opening on the

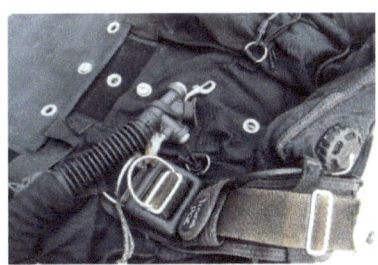

The swap – inflator at the hip and exhaust at the shoulder

Elbow pointing toward 2 o'clock

Oral inflation needs to be possible. If you can't reach it, you must get a longer corrugated hose.

Mesh screen used in exhaust valve

bottom of your wing, positioning the elbow so that it's pointing up and slightly out toward the left shoulder strap. When you are looking down at the rig in front of you, the elbow will point to about 2 o'clock when placed on the left side (as you're wearing it). If you place the inflator on the right, then it's 10 o'clock. Run the corrugated hose through bicycle innertube (you'll want to buy some of this, it's great for many applications) or bungee that's attached to the shoulder webbing. This will hold it in place. Finally, attach the power inflator to the chest strap, if you have one, with innertube or bungee. This holds it in place in the center of your chest for easy access. If you don't use a chest strap, you'll have to add a bolt snap so you can clip the power inflator to a chest D-ring on the opposite side. When you put your rig on, you should ensure that you can orally inflate with the inflator hose in this new position.

To install the new exhaust, cut the cord on the exhaust valve and remove it. Thread #24 cave line or similar through the hole in the top of the exhaust cover, and tie a knot on the end inside of the cover. You will need to pull the rubber disk out of the cover to get to the hole.

If the exhaust valve is on the outside of the wing, you may want to consider inserting a mesh screen inside the exhaust valve cover. I've had small pieces of limestone dislodged by bubbles percolating on the ceiling drop down and enter one of the openings at the exact right moment so they lodged in the exhaust valve and prevented it from closing. While you may not be diving in a cave, you might do a swim through or venture into a wreck, and the same thing can happen. When it happened to me, my wing was useless. Even blasting air into the wing while tugging on the dump cord did not dislodge the intruder. After the second occurrence, I bought some soft window screening. I used the exhaust cover as a template to cut out a circle. I then slit the circle half-way across from the outer perimeter to the center. I inserted the mesh screen into the exhaust valve cover so the two sides of the slit overlapped each other. It may be easier to insert the new cord through the center hole prior to inserting the screen. Screw the valve onto the opening on top of the wing, twisting it on slowly so the spring inside does not cause the mesh screen to bunch up on itself.

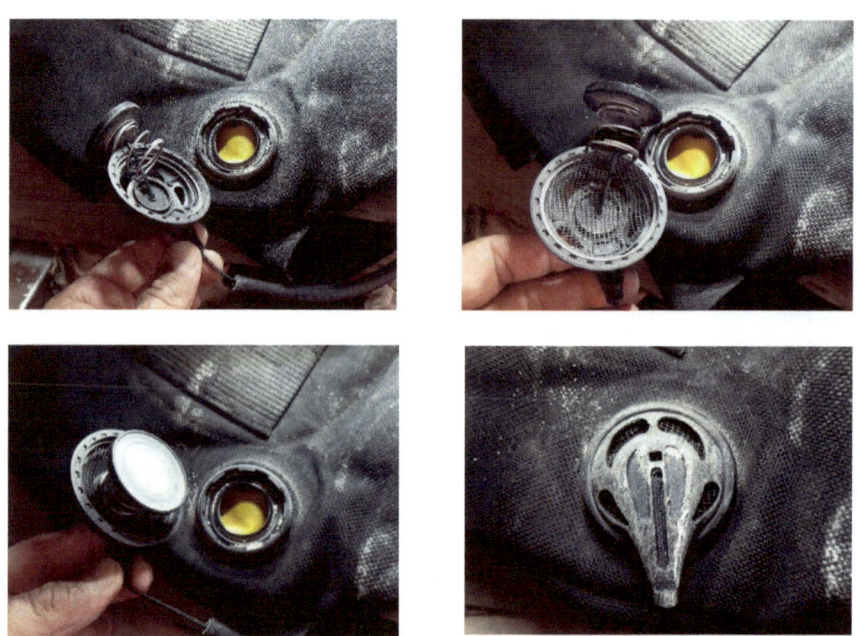

Exhaust valve removed from wing. Mesh screen inserted into exhaust valve cap. Tension maintained on spring to hold mesh screen in place. Exhaust valve screwed back on wing with mesh screen visible through all openings.

If you have a sidemount rig in which the shoulder port is on the inside of the wing against your back, inserting a screen won't be necessary. With the exhaust valve facing down, debris won't be able to enter and jam it open. However, this also means that you won't be able

Tubing held in place by the shoulder weight. Pull dump is in line with the D-ring

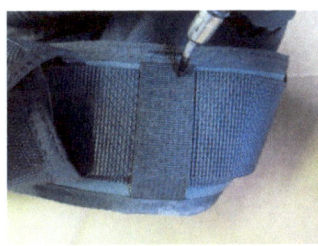

Burning a hole in the webbing so you can secure the tubing with small zip ties

to exhaust all the air out of the wing without getting vertical. This is one of the reasons the inside hip exhaust doesn't work well. Remember, air rises in water. If the exhaust port is on the side of the wing against your back, all of the air won't be able to escape from there.

Back to swapping the inflator and exhaust. Run the line along the shoulder strap from the exhaust valve and cut it about 2 inches/5 cm below the chest D-ring (the top one if you use two). You can leave the line as is or use a piece of tubing with an inner diameter slightly larger than the line (1/8 inch/3 mm is sufficient). This tubing can be found in the lawn sprinkler section of your local hardware store. The tubing needs to run from about 1 inch/2.5 cm from where the line exits the exhaust valve to where you want to position the end of the pull dump. Cut the tubing the proper length and thread the line through it. The tubing helps keep the line in the same place so it is easily accessible whenever you need it. Either way, you'll end up securing the line or the tubing.

You want to secure the line or tubing so it stays in the same location at all times and is easy to find once you build the muscle memory. You can use some bicycle inner tube or a loop of bungee, thread it around the shoulder harness, and run the line or tube through the innertube or bungee. Or you can secure it to the webbing with zip ties. Using a soldering iron or wood burner, burn two to three holes near the edge of the shoulder harness webbing. Attach the tubing to the harness using small zip ties. Thread the end of the cord through your pull dump knob, pull the exhaust open, and tie a knot in the cord close to the knob. Let the cord relax to make sure the exhaust valve doesn't remain open. You need to determine the proper cord length with the rig on. While the cord might seem long enough with the rig resting on the table in front of you, once your shoulders fill it out, it tends to get too short and keep the exhaust valve open. If the valve can close with the rig on, cut the excess line off. You are now done with the inflator/exhaust swap.

A final consideration when placing the exhaust valve at the shoulder is whether the opening is on the outside of the wing or the inside against your back. If it's located below the wing, against your back, you will have to be aware of the potential for the line to be stuck between the wing and your exposure suit with the valve in an open position. With cylinders hanging from your rig exerting downward pressure on it, the line can get wedged with the valve open. This means when you try to inflate, the air will escape through the open exhaust valve. I've witnessed this numerous times and had to assist students and buddies by reaching between the wing and shoulder to release the tension on the line enough to allow the exhaust valve to close.

Zip ties holding tubing in position along the shoulder strap. They need to be snug but not too tight otherwise they will pinch the line, making it difficult to pull and release.

New shoulder exhaust installation completed. Note the zip ties securing the tubing in place.

Another thing to watch for is wear and tear on the line. With it in this position, because you are pulling it laterally rather than straight out, the line will wear down and need to be replaced every few months (depending on how often you dive). If you use zip ties to secure the tubing, you may need to replace it as well because it can be difficult to thread the line through it once it's been secured with zip ties.

Pillow Shaped Wings

Because of the different design of pillow shaped wings, the inflator and exhaust ports come in a variety of positions. On some, you will still have the ports located at the shoulder or center of the upper back and the hip areas just like with the horseshoe and donut shaped wings. However, the inflator will already be located at the hip and the exhaust at the shoulder. In this situation, you may just need to add a screen to the exhaust valve to keep debris from being able to jam it open.

Pillow shaped wing with the inflator and exhaust both located on the inside bottom at the sides of the wing

Other pillow shaped wings have the ports located on either side of the wing. The wing is typically wide enough that it follows the contour of your back and positions the ports at your sides. Inserting a screen in the exhaust valve located on the outside is still recommended.

Something to consider is which side you want the inflator and which side the exhaust. If you only dive during daylight hours, this won't make much of a difference. However, if you dive at night, you will want to give this some thought. Having the exhaust valve behind you requires you to reach back to find the cord and pull it. If you carry a light strapped to your hand, you don't want to reach back with your light in your hand, especially if you have other divers behind you. If you do this, you will likely shine the beam in their eyes and cause momentary blindness. Sure, you can grab the light with your other hand before you reach back, but you might be doing this quite a bit during a dive. The alternative is to position the inflator on the same side as your light hand so your empty hand is free to reach back and pull the exhaust cord on the other side as needed.

Pillow shaped wing with the inflator and exhaust both located on the outside bottom at the sides of the wing

Pillow shaped wing with the inflator and exhaust located on the outside center of the sides of the wing

Hybrid wing with exhaust valve located at bottom center of wing and inflator on the upper left side with the opposite side sealed

There is also a pillow shaped wing that comes with the exhaust port in the bottom center of the wing. There are two inflator ports, one located on each side on the outer part of the wing at the side near the top. The option is there to place the inflator hose on either side with the opposite side remaining sealed. In this case, it doesn't matter which side you place the inflator because you can exhaust air with either hand. The central location of the exhaust allows you to reach back with either hand to release air. The only modification I recommend for this positioning is inserting a screen into the exhaust valve.

Wing customizations

One of the things that must be done to keep a sidemount rig streamlined and trimmed is to keep the wing as flat as possible on your back. It doesn't matter what style wing you have. Unfortunately, most rigs don't come this way out of the bag and will need some modifications. Some sidemount rigs come with the lower area of the wing not secured tightly enough to the harness to keep that area of the wing from riding up. The horseshoe and donut shaped wings typically attach the lower sides of the wings to the waist strap with sliders, but these have free movement along the webbing. The purpose of the sliders is to allow the wing to fully inflate and create more lift. However, they are allowed too much movement and the sides of the wing will taco, creating a higher than necessary profile.

The easiest way to address the sliders on these wings is by locking them in place with triglides. By securing the slider into a triglide, the wing stretches flat across your waist, providing a more streamlined rig. Yes, you will lose a little bit of lift by doing this, but most wings come with far too much lift anyway.

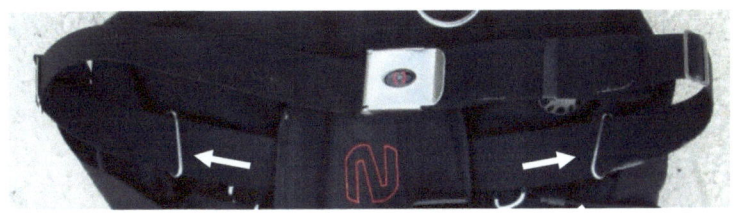

Wing sliders on waist strap allow too much movement and the wing tends to taco when partially inflated.

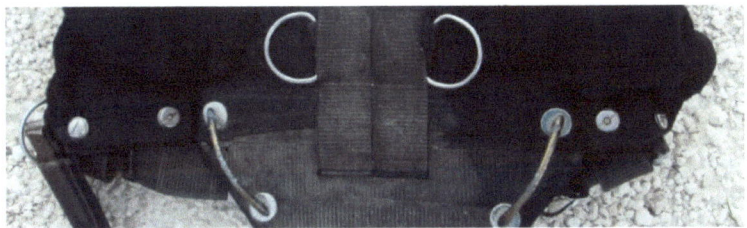

Wing locked in place on waist strap with sex bolts

Wing slider locked in place by triglide keeps the wing laterally stretched, preventing it from sliding back and creating a taco effect when it is partially inflated.

Fortunately, most sidemount rigs are not like this. Some rigs come with the bottom of the wing bolted to the waist strap. This holds the wing in place and keeps it flat at the bottom. Other rigs have the wings permanently sewn onto the waist strap. There are also wings that are designed to be stretched out across the back without attachments to the harness. Be aware of these differences when shopping for sidemount rigs.

Many pillow shaped wings are not designed with the edges of the bottom of the wing attached to the harness. Instead, they use belly bands to place tension across the wing and stretch it over the back. The wings still need to be stretched along the spine as well, though. When you are evaluating sidemount rigs, make sure the top and bottom of the pillow shaped wings are secured enough to keep the wing flat.

All sidemount rigs will have a way for the wing to be attached to the spine of the harness. This is usually done by attaching the top to the shoulder plate and the bottom to the lumbar plate. However, it's not always snug enough to hold the wing down when there's air in it. This is another time when bungee is useful. Secure the bottom of the wing to the spine or crotch strap of the harness by wrapping it 3-4 times around the wing and harness webbing, making sure the bungee is flush against the edge of the wing. Another option is to have them sewn together, but this will make it so the harness is no longer adjustable.

Another issue with systems using longer horseshoe and donut shaped wings that can occur involves the attachment of the top of the wing to the shoulder straps. These wings are longer than pillow shaped wings and wider at the top, so rather than being attached to the shoulder plate, they are attached to the shoulder straps. This attachment is usually done with a tab that the shoulder webbing is threaded through to hold the strap in place over the wing. The issue is that the top of the wing can ride down on the shoulder strap when the rig is donned.

When you first get your brand new rig, you won't notice this. The material is new and stiff, so it will hold its form. After several dives, the exposure to water will soften the material and it will eventually start to travel down and create an air entrapment at the top of the wing. The shoulder straps on these rigs are usually made up of 2 inch/5 cm webbing that is

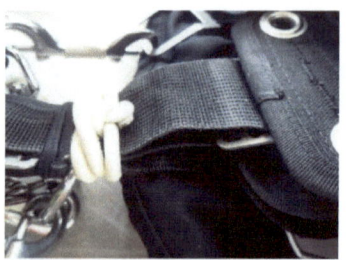

Modification necessary to keep wing from floating up at the bottom. Top shows the underside of the wing. Bottom shows the top view. Note the bungee is flush against the edge of the wing.

Wing tab at top of wing locked in place by triglide in between the 2 pieces of shoulder webbing preventing the top of the wing from riding down.

Bungee inside wing

Bungee secured through tab with a knot to the inside to keep the upper wing stretched out

Belly band attached to tabs used to stretch the mid portion of the wing

folded over on itself and held together with a triglide. There's an easy fix for the issue. Route the upper wing tab between the two pieces of shoulder webbing on the front side of the triglide. This will hold the wing in place when it is donned.

If there is not enough webbing to do this, or the design of the wing and harness doesn't allow for this, you can secure the tab to a triglide with bungee. Create a loop of bungee around the tab and thread it through the triglide to hold it in place. If you choose not to make this customization, be sure to pull up on the wing after donning it to ensure it is stretched out and will not trap air.

Finally, we need to look at the overall wing. Horseshoe and donut shaped wings typically come with bungee on the underside looped through tabs on the outer and inner edges. This bungee is supposed to pull the outside of the wing in so it doesn't taco as much. If it's tight enough, it does help pull the edges of the wing in toward the center, but the topside of the wing isn't stretched so it's still not flat when it is partially inflated.

There's a fairly easy fix for this. The tabs are already there to secure the inner bungee. To keep the topside of the wing from rising, feed the bungee used to hold the cylinder valves through tabs that are positioned just below your armpits. You will need to knot the bungee to the inside of the tab so it can pull the tab down against your back. This will keep the edges of the top of the wing stretched out.

The bottom and top of the wing are held down now, but the middle section still rises up. There should be another tab midway on the wing. This tab can be used to hold a belly band. A belly band is a bungee attached to each side of the wing that straps across your belly and is secured in place by a piece of hardware. You can use a double ender, a standard bolt snap, or a bungee holder. To make a belly band, create two bungee loops that measure from the side of your ribs to the center of your abdomen. Insert one end of each loop through the tabs on the wing. When you don the rig, you will clip the two free ends together with your hardware of choice.

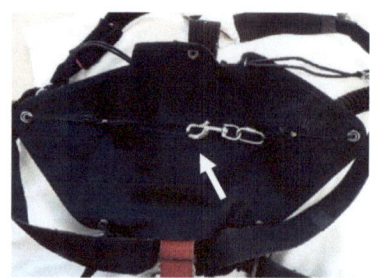

Belly band used to pull down the edges of a smaller wing

Although belly bands can be used with any type of wing, they are more common in pillow shaped wings. Pillow shaped wings tend to bulge up in the middle when they are inflated. If they are not quite full, they will bulge more than when they are full. This is because filling the wing works to stretch it across your back. But how often will you have your wing completely full?

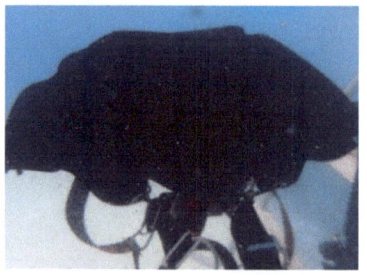

Fully inflated pillow shaped wing (top) versus a partially inflated pillow shaped wing (bottom). Both wings are being stretched out by a belly band, but the partially inflated wing still has a higher profile than the fully inflated wing.

Some manufacturers have placed baffles in their wings to try to counteract this, but the baffles only do so much. The key to keeping these wings as flat as possible is to stretch them out across the back. This is done with belly bands. I use belly bands with my pillow shaped wings and my horseshoe shaped wing.

Because of the need to attach the wing to the harness, most pillow shaped wings come with grommets along the

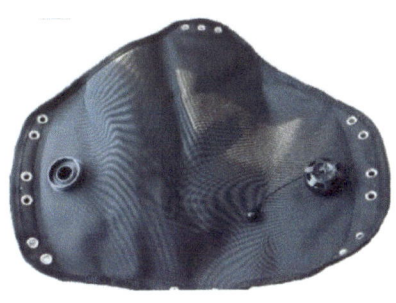

The side of this wing has 6 grommets each to allow attachment of 3 belly bands, each band using 2 grommet holes. This keeps the wing flatter against the back when partially inflated.

edges. These grommets are there so bungee can be used to secure the wing to the harness. The wing shown to the left has grommets at the top to secure the wing to the shoulder plate and grommets at the bottom to secure it to the crotch strap. You can see six grommets on each side of the wing. These are for belly bands. You'll find most wings have only one or two grommets on each side. Smaller pillow shaped wings can get away with less. However, as the wing gets larger, it requires more belly bands to keep it sufficiently flat. Most larger wings come with only two grommets on each side, but that allows the center of the wing to rise. Spacing the grommets closer to each other will result in a much flatter wing. Because there is tension placed along the entire edge of the wing, it is sufficiently stretched to remain flat when partially inflated.

These are many of the common wing modifications being made to sidemount rigs. I'm sure there are more out there because sidemount divers are always tweaking their rigs trying to find better ways. Some modifications may work for you. Others may not. Try various methods and experiment with your own modifications until you find something that works for your diving.

8 CUSTOMIZING YOUR SIDEMOUNT RIG
HARNESS MODIFICATIONS

Harness modifications

View of trapped light from the front. The light can be unclipped & pulled out but restowing it is difficult.

View of trapped light from the back. Placement can interfere with the orientation of the cylinder.

Sidemount rigs generally have one of two standard harness routings – the V routing, in which the webbing of the shoulder harness routes down and to the back of the waist strap (similar to Hogarthian backplate harness routing), and the H routing, in which the shoulder straps route directly down the front of the torso to the front of the waist strap rather than back to the spine. There are advantages and disadvantages to both. Let's look at the simple ones first.

A common way for divers to store small dive lights is on the shoulder webbing under the D-rings. This works fine with the cylinders mounted on the back. However, with the cylinders mounted on the side, the backup lights can get trapped underneath the cylinder valves with the V routing. This not only makes it difficult to deploy them, but it also increases the chance of affecting the trim of the sidemount cylinders by pushing the valves into rotation.

You can relocate the lights or you can convert to an H harness. Because the shoulder webbing on the H harness routes down and not under the cylinders, it allows lights to be stored on the shoulder webbing without trapping them or affecting cylinder trim. Is it worth changing routing because of backup lights? Maybe, maybe not. It's a personal preference. You can always store the lights up along the harness above the D-rings. Or you can store them in pockets.

The more important difference between the harness routings is stability. In the V harness, you have six points of the harness all coming off of one plate on the back. The shoulder straps, waist straps, spine, and crotch strap all join at the lumbar plate over the lower back of the rig. All tension created by the rig is thus coming off of this one point. This is not a major issue with aluminum cylinders and lighter steel cylinders. Aluminum cylinders basically float alongside the diver and do not put significant weight or tension on the harness. The harness essentially holds the wing and hardware in place with only slight tension on it being created by the cylinders.

V harness – all the webbing converges to one point.

In contrast to the V harness, the H harness doesn't concentrate tension in one area. The lumbar plate at the lower back only has the waist, spine, and crotch straps coming off of it. There is tension created laterally by the waist straps and tension created vertically by the spine and crotch straps. The shoulder straps are routed from the top of the spine, over the shoulders, and straight down to the waist straps. The shoulder straps are creating an upward force on the spine and the front of the waist. The upward force on the waist is counteracted by a downward force created by the crotch strap. We'll discuss the importance of this in chapter 9.

H harness – tension is distributed evenly on the harness.

This difference gives the H harness routing an advantage in handling heavier steel cylinders that place more tension and weight on the it. V harness rigs are more prone to get off balance by slipping to one side or the other. Because all of the tension is placed on the lumbar plate located at the lower rear of the harness, heavier steel cylinders can cause the harness to shift and this can affect trim. This isn't as likely with the H harness routing. The counteracting forces of the shoulder and crotch straps add stability to the H harness. It's also easier to tell if the harness

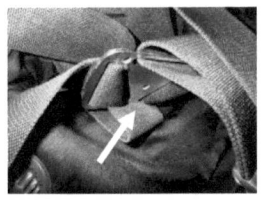

is off center with the H harness. You can feel or look at the shoulder straps and see if they are shifted to one side or the other when they are in front of you, something you can't do when they are secured to the lumbar plate.

Shoulder & waist straps are continuous & can slide through the lumbar plate slots.

Another issue with the V harness is that the shoulder and waist straps are one continuous piece. If the webbing isn't secured in place at the lumbar plate, it can slide through and make the shoulder straps uneven in length, which will result in a less stable rig. This can be addressed by threading a triglide onto the webbing to keep it from being able to slide through the plate.

Converting a V Harness to an H Harness

If you're dealing with just the harness, converting from a V to an H isn't difficult. You will need additional triglides and enough webbing to create a waist strap. If your rig is one in which the harness and wing are one system sewn together, it will be a little more involved.

The first thing to do is remove the hardware from the waist strap and pull the ends of the webbing out of the lumbar plate. This will leave you with very long shoulder straps. You will either need to have sufficiently long webbing for a waist strap or shift the shoulder webbing so one end is long enough to form a shoulder strap and cut the excess from the opposite end.

Take the webbing you have for the belt and feed it through the vertical slots you just removed the other webbing from to form the new waist strap. Place the harness over your shoulders with the waist strap around your waist. Hang the shoulder straps down in front of you. Mark these straps about 6 inches/15 cm below the bottom of the waist strap. Remove the harness and cut the webbing at your marks, making sure to burn the edges to keep them from fraying. Now fold the webbing back on itself 6 inches/15 cm from the ends.

Next, you need to replace the hardware as well as add some hardware to create the H harness. First place any rear and side D-rings onto the new waist strap. You'll need an additional triglide on each side. These will be placed on the webbing just to the outside of where the shoulder straps will meet the waist strap. Their purpose is to keep the shoulder straps from sliding along the waist. You can also add D-rings here if needed to use with aluminum cylinders.

Place a triglide on each of the shoulder straps so they are positioned 2 ¼ inches/57mm from the fold. Form a loop around the waist strap with the end to the inside of the waist strap and feed the end through the triglides. The loop should be small enough so that it sits snugly on the waist strap and is fixed in place by triglides. You can place a narrow loop of bicycle innertube just above the triglide to keep the loose end flush against the front of the strap. One of these can also be used to secure the corrugated inflator hose to the harness. Finish the conversion by sliding triglides onto the waist strap to secure the inside of the shoulder straps in place and thread on the buckle. See Appendix C for detailed instructions with photos of the H harness shoulder webbing attachments to the waist strap webbing.

Rather than forming loops to secure the ends of the shoulder straps, there is hardware you can use that allows the waist and shoulder straps to be threaded perpendicular to each other. Slide the hardware into position on the waist strap as you would a triglide. Then thread the shoulder straps through the slots at the top of the hardware. Hardware is now available that gives you the option of directing the shoulder straps at an angle or straight up. The angled hardware allows you to position the shoulder straps slightly to the side rather than straight down your chest and abdomen.

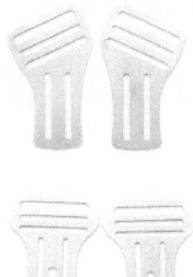

Hardware designed to secure shoulder webbing to waist webbing, angled and straight

You now have an H harness. You will want to position the shoulder straps so they are coming straight down from your shoulders to your waist. If you use the same harness for recreational tropical warm water diving and cold dry suit diving, you can adjust the triglides and shoulder webbing or specialized hardware by sliding them along the waist strap to reposition the shoulder straps and accommodate the added thickness of the suit and undergarments.

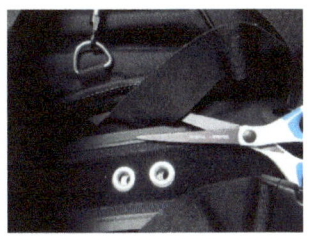

When cutting shoulder webbing on V harness, make sure you cut it as close to the stitch as possible to allow for sufficient length to form the shoulder straps.

Converting a one-piece V Harness to an H Harness

Converting a one-piece rig from one type of harness to the other is a little more involved than pulling the webbing out of hardware to reroute it. Some of these rigs are sewn together, so you will have to cut the shoulder straps where they attach at the back of the harness/wing. Cut them as close as you can to the stitch line to leave yourself enough length to form the loop at the front of the rig or route them through the hardware. Once you have the free ends, follow the instructions above to secure the shoulder straps to the waist strap. Remove the buckles and any front D-rings on the waist strap to get ready to place the shoulder strap loops or hardware over the waist strap.

V harness with slider used to secure the shoulder/waist strap to the back. Unthread the webbing. When creating the new waist strap, remember to use triglides to lock the webbing in place at the sliders.

You may also come across one-piece sidemount rigs that are not sewn and do not incorporate a lumbar plate. The crotch strap is sewn to the wing and the shoulder and waist strap are threaded through a slider. With these, simply unthread the webbing to create the new shoulder straps. If you use the loop method, remember to place triglides on each side of the sliders to prevent it from moving from side to side.

Chest Strap

Not everyone uses a chest strap with a sidemount rig, but they do have a couple of advantages. A chest strap provides a location to secure the power inflator at mid-chest for easy access should you need to orally inflate. It also helps keep the shoulder straps in place rather than allowing them to migrate out toward your arms.

The common chest straps that come with some sidemount rigs are the adjustable 1 inch/2.5 cm webbing straps. These straps use a buckle to hold the two ends together. At first, new out of the bag, they are stiff enough to do what they are designed to do and remain the length you set them. After several dives, the webbing loses its stiffness and starts to slide through the buckles freely. While they may start out where you want them, by the end of the dive they are stretched out completely and you've lost stability in the shoulder straps.

Adjustable 1 inch/2.5 cm chest strap

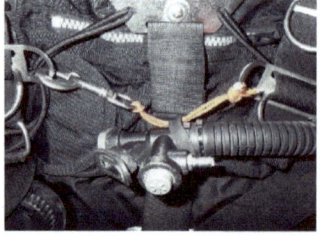

Static line chest strap with bolt snap

An easy fix to this is for remove these and replace them with a static cord tied into a large loop with a bolt snap on one end. Loop the other end through a D-ring on the same side as your corrugated hose. You can then secure the power inflator to the chest strap with bicycle innertube or bungee. The strap will always be the same length.

D-Rings

How many D-rings do you need? Like most other things in sidemount, that will be a matter of personal preference as well as how you rig things and what you're carrying. Let's start with the chest D-rings. Most rigs manufactured with steel cylinders in mind come standard with two chest D-rings on each shoulder strap. In contrast, the rigs manufactured with aluminum cylinders in mind tend to come standard with only one chest D-ring on each side. This doesn't mean you need to keep it this way. D-rings can be removed or added. There are advantages to both configurations. One D-ring on each side reduces clutter on the chest...in most cases. There are two less D-rings, so things are less

Modified chest strap holding power inflator in place

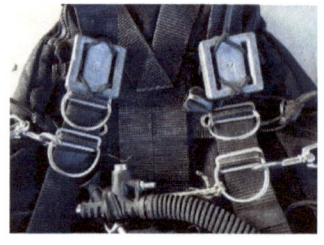

Chest D-rings – whether you have 2 or 1 on each side is a personal preference.

If your wing does not cover the waist strap you can use standard D-rings on the waist as well as offset D-rings.

Offset D-rings on rear of rig when there isn't a place for D-rings on the waist.

Waist D-rings on the front

busy. However, if you are using the chest D-rings for multiple items of gear, then having only two can actually increase clutter.

Let's say you store your dive lights on the chest straps and you use bolt snaps on leashes on the cylinder necks. You now have two bolt snaps clipped onto the D-ring on each side as your standard. Add to that clipping your 2nd stage regulators and things can get confusing. Also, if you choose to route your 2nd stage regulator hoses directly to your mouth, you'll need D-rings higher on your shoulders where it's not practical to clip anything else other than the 2nd stage. In these cases, a second D-ring on each side might be helpful. With two D-rings on each side, you can clip items you are unlikely to have to use, such as your dive lights and cylinder neck bolt snaps to the lower D-rings. You then use the upper D-rings exclusively for items that are clipped on and off throughout the dive, such as your 2nd stages.

What about D-rings on the waist? As far as D-rings on the back of the rig, this will depend on whether your wing covers your waist strap or not and whether you use a butt plate. For smaller wings that are positioned above the waist strap, additional D-rings may be useful. You will obviously need a D-ring on each side to clip your cylinders. Additional D-rings may also be useful to clip canister lights, spools/reels and surface marker buoys (SMBs), pouches, and any other items you may need. The more you have to clip, the more D-rings you may want (reasonably so) to make it easier to access the items. There are also pieces of hardware with offset D-rings that can be very useful, especially when the wing covers the waist strap or when you want some additional D-rings on the crotch strap.

Experiment with the D-rings and their positions and use what works best for you and what you're carrying. And keep in mind, there can be a fine line between having enough D-rings and having too many or too few.

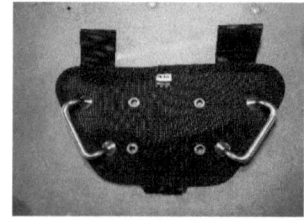

Add-on butt plate with offset rails. Secured to the waist strap using the tabs at the top.

Butt plate modifications

The final topic of harness modifications we'll cover is the butt plate. The butt plate is typically used with steel cylinders as an attachment point for the body of the cylinders. They have rails attached to the sides for this purpose.

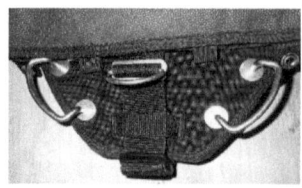

Smaller butt plate with curved offset rails. Offset rails are typically used to make them easier to reach.

Butt plate rails come in different shapes. They can be straight or curved, standard or offset. Most sidemount systems that use butt plates come with offset rails at the time of this writing, but that's always subject to change. Just because your rig comes with a particular style rail doesn't mean you have to keep it. They are easily changed with a quick trip to your local hardware store.

The purpose of the offset rail is to extend it out to the side so that it is easier to reach while clipping on cylinders. This is especially necessary with narrow butt plates where the rails are more difficult to reach. The issue with the offset rails is that they don't stabilize the cylinders as well as standard rails. The curved rails provide even less stability than the straight ones.

Standard, straight rails on narrow butt plate can be difficult to reach.

When you get in the water, you want to position your cylinders so they hang from your rig at your sides with the valves just below your armpits. The valves are hanging from bungees that serve to hold them up. The bolt snap on the body of the cylinder is supposed to hold

Standard, straight rails that were sold as drawer pulls at the hardware store

Standard, curved rails that were sold as drawer pulls at the hardware store

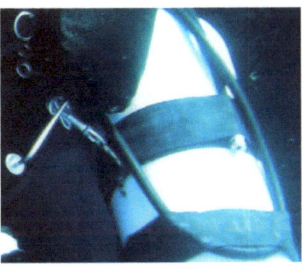

Bolt snap locked in at the top of the rail. Because the bolt snap slides down the leg of the rail against the butt plate, it typically remains in that position.

Curved offset rails don't allow the bolt snap to lock into the top of the rail even with the legs. This allows the bolt snap to slide along the rail and the cylinder to easily change position.

the cylinder in place along your body. We do this by pulling the cylinders forward so they sit just inside our armpits once we are horizontal in the water. The bolt snaps on the rails then lock into place at the top of the rail.

The bolt snap is not able to do this with the offset rails, especially the curved offset rails. On the offset rails, the bolt snap slides freely along the long end of the rail. If you always maintain a perfectly horizontal trim on your dive, this isn't much of an issue. However, if you end up in a head up position, because you are swimming along a slope for instance, this will allow the bolt snap to slide down along the rail. This small shift in the position of the cylinders can be enough to throw your trim off and make you foot heavy until you pull the cylinders back up to return the bolt snaps to the top of the rails. With the standard rails, the bolt snap usually stays in place.

If the sidemount rig you like has offset rails, all you have to do is measure the rails and head to the cabinet hardware section of your local hardware store. Find a drawer pull with the same measurement and grab two. Then head to the screw section to find shorter screws to affix your new rails to your butt plate. You may be able to reuse the screws from the stock rails. However, they might be a different diameter or thread.

This not only wraps it up for harness modifications but for all modifications of your sidemount system. Now we'll move onto preparing to get in the water with your new sidemount rig.

9 ACHIEVING PROPER TRIM IN SIDEMOUNT
BEFORE GETTING WET

The biggest mistake made in sidemount diving is not positioning cylinders correctly. Many divers think all they have to do is clip the cylinders on and they're ready to go. This typically results in more of a slinging of the cylinders below the body than along the sides. It's also what some people refer to as front mounting. This can result in some divers hating sidemount the first time in the water and never trying it again. Some keep working at it and fighting it and never really liking it. Others get the cylinders positioned somewhat decently and become used to it. Unfortunately, it is not uncommon to see divers whose cylinders are not located in the optimal position.

The idea behind sidemount diving is to be streamlined and to create a smaller profile. Even though there are divers who dive sidemount for the benefit of not having to carry more than 100 pounds/45 kilograms of weight on their back on land, striving for near perfect trim in the water in order to reduce resistance while swimming should still be an objective. You will find that you enjoy the dive much more with the cylinders well-trimmed. This doesn't mean that they need to be perfect all of the time. If you're constantly working to maintain perfect trim, what fun are you having? Scuba diving is meant to be fun, isn't it?

Well-trimmed sidemount diver

The ideal position for sidemount cylinders is parallel and on an even plane with the body. While this may feel uncomfortable to some at first, it's not so much a matter of comfort as it is a matter of being different. D-rings are in different locations. The cylinders can feel obtrusive in their new locations. Some of this could be a result of poor positioning. Most of it is a result of new equipment in a new location. It will take time in the new configuration for the new sidemount diver to get used to it.

One of the things that immensely helps with proper positioning of the cylinders is to get video or photo feedback. You need to see what the rig and cylinders look like on your body. It's not enough to get feedback from someone, even an instructor or experienced mentor. You need to look at yourself so you can associate the look with the feeling you have in the water. This doesn't mean you have to spend a small fortune on an underwater camera system. There are "snorkeling" cameras available that are waterproof to shallow depths (10-15 feet/3-4.5 meters) and cost as little as $15 USD. You don't have to go deep to get these photos. In fact, shallow is better. It gives you more time in the water, more ambient light, and helps you work on your buoyancy control. The slightest changes in the first atmosphere of depth result in significant changes in buoyancy. If you can properly control your buoyancy in shallow water, you will have no issues controlling it in deeper water. And seeing a photo can make all the difference when working on your trim.

Several years ago, I had a student in the water doing drills, and he was not happy with his position. He insisted his head was too low. He became upset because I told him his trim looked fine. He thought I was lying to him. I had taken several photos of him during the dive and showed him what he looked like on the display of the camera right there in the water. Only then did his attitude change. He told me if it wasn't for the photos, he would never have believed he was not head down.

The problem was that the isolator valve on the twinset cylinders he was used to diving kept him from being able to raise his head and he had to position himself with his shoulders slightly up to see forward. This is standard when diving with a backmounted cylinder. With no isolator behind his head, he could raise his head to see forward. This allowed him to place his body in a more horizontal position, which resulted in his shoulders and head being lower than he was used to, so it felt like he was head down. He's not the only student that has expressed this feeling.

Getting the harness ready

Before you get in the water with your sidemount rig, you need to

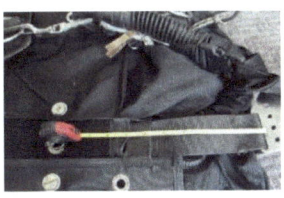

Measuring the waist strap is important to ensure the wing is stretched evenly on both sides.

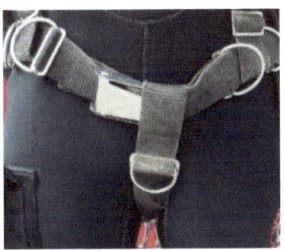

Crotch strap pulling down on waist strap against the shoulder straps

make sure everything is set up evenly on the rig. If you have a sidemount rig where the lower portions of the wing are attached to the waist strap with sliders, make sure they are even. The easiest way to do this is to measure the waist strap from the edge of the plate to the edge of the wing attachment where it is secured to the waist strap.

This measurement needs to be perfect. Even a ¼ inch/5 mm difference can be enough to throw your trim off. Having the wing off by that much can cause a list to one side. Yes, this is true! A buddy of mine had a listing problem and asked me to look at his rig. Everything looked fine at first glance. Then I pulled out the tape measure and started measuring. The triglides where the wing was attached to the waist strap were off by a ¼ inch/5 mm. I didn't believe this was the issue, but I couldn't find any other problem, so I made the adjustment. We returned to the water to see if the adjustment made any difference. He was no longer listing to one side.

I gave this some thought because it didn't seem like that small of a discrepancy should cause such an issue. What was happening to cause the list was the longer side was stretching the wing on that side and reducing the space available in the wing. Because air in water rises and travels the path of least resistance, the air in the wing will migrate to the opposite side where the wing isn't as cinched down. So more air remains on one side than the other and creates more buoyancy on that side. Keeping the wing stretched out evenly on both sides will cause air in the bladder to distribute evenly and keep the rig from listing to either side. This is true for any type of wing. This is why making sure the waist strap doesn't slide back and forth is so important.

Once the wing and straps are adjusted evenly, you need to adjust the crotch strap. The crotch strap should be just long enough so that it's pulling down on the waist strap. This gives you optimal stability in your rig. This was mentioned in the discussion about the H harness in chapter

8. The crotch strap is placing downward tension to oppose the upward tension created by the shoulder straps. This helps keep the back of the harness snug so the wing is stretched from top to bottom. It also gives you a more stable harness by having opposing tension on the waist strap. The added stability is useful when using steel sidemount cylinders that place more tension on the harness. The crotch strap actually has a function. Having the crotch strap simply held in place on the waist strap or hanging loosely between your thighs will keep the strap in place, but it doesn't do much to hold the rest of the rig in place.

While you are adjusting the length of the crotch strap, make sure the rear D-ring is positioned about mid-buttocks area. Most divers have difficulty reaching anything clipped onto the rear crotch strap D-ring if it is any lower. Start with it midway and adjust its location so it works for you. This may mean modifying the butt plate to add a D-ring.

On this rig, the butt plate is too long to make a D-ring below it useful. A D-ring was added at the offset D-rings where it can be reached easily.

If you made any adjustments to the shoulder straps and chest D-rings, make sure they are even with each other as well. This isn't as much of an issue if you have adjustable shoulder straps. However, it might be noticeable if the D-rings are not even. If you have shoulder straps that are not easily adjustable with the rig on, then it is important to make sure they are equal lengths before getting in the water.

The Cylinders

Now let's look at the cylinders. The different options on how to set up the cylinders involve which way the valve opening faces when in the water and horizontal - down, up, in or out. The first thing to consider is where the handwheels are positioned. Most divers like the handwheels pointing out away from them. This provides the easiest access in case you need to close a valve for any reason. Some divers prefer to have the handwheels pointing forward. This does place the handwheels in a position for accessing them with either hand. You could also point the handwheels in toward your chest, but this makes it more difficult to reach when opening and closing the valve.

Curb feeler used on cars decades ago

SPG up or down

Note the position of the HP hoses coming from the armpits and SPGs pushed against the shoulders.

SPG positioned down alongside the cylinder

Before you decide how you want to position your valves, you need to decide where you want to position the submersible pressure gauges (SPGs)/transmitters. This will help determine which way to position the 1st stages. There is something to consider with this decision. Many 1st stages have high pressure (HP) ports that are slightly angled away from the DIN or yoke connector. While this works well with cylinders worn on the back by directing the HP hose forward toward the diver, in sidemount it will cause the SPG to point out slightly when the 1st stages are facing forward. In this position, the 1st stages stick out below the diver and are much less streamlined. The diver essentially has curb feelers on. This isn't an issue with angled valves, but most cylinder valves are not angled.

There are a couple of easy solutions to the curb feeler issue. The SPGs can either be positioned on the 1st stages so they are routed down along the sides of the cylinders, or the valves can be faced back toward the shoulders so the 1st stages are set in the armpits. With the valves facing up, the high pressure hoses and SPGs will press against the front of the shoulders rather than sticking out and down. This still allows you to pull the SPG face out to check the pressure. It also acts somewhat as a gauge to check the trim of your cylinders. If the SPG begins to stick out from your shoulder too far, then you know the bottom of your cylinder is riding too high.

You can also position the SPGs alongside the cylinders. This works with the valves facing down or up. This is also the best position to place transmitters. With the valves facing up, you will have to reach around to the top of your cylinders to grab the SPGs and look back at them. You may also have to push the cylinders down slightly to be able to read the SPGs. With the SPGs alongside the front of the cylinders, they will be easier to access and read. Another advantage to having the 1st stages up is that they are protected.

If you have angled valves, the only way to orient the 1st stages with SPGs is to have the valve opening facing down. The angle of the valve will place the SPG too far forward with the opening facing up, and you'll have curb feelers. With the opening facing down, the SPG is pushed against the shoulder.

Once you have decided on 1st stage position, you need to place the cam bands or worm gear clamps on the cylinders so that the bolt snaps or carabiners are in the appropriate position. The position of the bolt snaps depends on a variety of factors – whether you're using steel or aluminum cylinders, the sidemount system you use, and the position of the rear attachment points on your rig. The most common positions for the bolt snaps are at 3 o'clock and 9 o'clock for the right and left cylinders, respectively, or 2 o'clock and 10 o'clock.

With aluminum cylinders or very light steel cylinders that require the bungee to route around the neck and may need the clip to be relocated from the rear to the front, or if you use sliding D-rings, 3 and 9 are the optimal position for the clips. This centers the pivot point on the cylinders whether they are clipped to the rear or front of the waist strap. For heavier steel cylinders, 2 and 10 tend to work well for most divers as the cylinders hang from the rear attachment the entire dive and the valve bungee typically puts some rotation on the cylinder. However, the thinner you are, or the farther out your attachment points on your back, the more likely you'll end up using the 3 and 9 positions. This is because the 2 and 10 positions place

Typical position for bolt snaps on cylinders.

3 o'clock on the left and 9 o'clock on the right (black lines)

An alternative would be 2 and 10 (red)

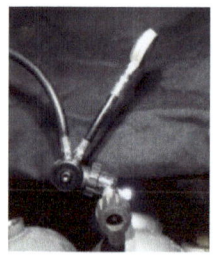

Angled valve with SPG must face forward so the SPG is pushed against the shoulder and not down in front of the diver creating a curb feeler.

96

The clip on the cam band needs to be even with the top of the butt plate rail or D-ring it attaches to.

Perfect position of the cam band

Note the angle of the leashes. These bands are positioned too low causing the need for longer leashes.

the bolt snaps higher on the cylinders and in turn allows the cylinders to hang too low on thinner divers, even with no leash.

Once you have chosen the location of the bolt snap, you need to slide the cam bands or worm gear clamps onto the cylinders and place them in the proper position along the length of the cylinders. Ideally, you want the leashes on the bolt snaps to be as short as possible while still allowing you to be able to grasp them to clip them on and off. This means if you dive cold water with dry gloves, you may need a bit more leash than someone who dives bare handed. The shorter the leash, the more stable the cylinders will be, especially when you have to rotate to one side or the other.

To create a more stable configuration by using shorter cords on the bolt snaps, the bands/clamps should be positioned on the cylinders in line with the location on the rig where they will be attached. The easiest way to do this is to put the rig on and place the cylinder on a chair or table or truck tailgate. Place the cylinder so that the valve/1st stage is in your armpit where it would be when diving and reach back to where the clip will attach to the butt plate or a D-ring on your waist belt. This is where the band/clamp should be positioned on the cylinder.

Some divers believe that if you are foot heavy, moving the cam band or worm gear clamp lower on the cylinders will correct this issue. This is not true! The first part of the cylinder that needs to be positioned is the valve. The valve and 1st stage need to be in your armpit. Any farther forward places the valve in front of your shoulder forcing the cylinder out of trim. Moving the clamps/bands lower on your cylinders only works if the cylinders are moved forward along your body. The cylinders can only be positioned so far forward along the body without being in front of the shoulders. Any farther forward and they will be thrown out of trim.

The idea behind lowering the band/clamp is that the weight of the cylinder is redistributed farther forward. While this may be the case, it's not enough of a redistribution to make a difference. It only causes you to have to use longer leashes, reducing the stability of the cylinders, and pulls the cylinders forward so you are either out of trim or have to constantly push the cylinders back under your armpits. And you'll still be foot heavy! So the attachment point on the body of the cylinder does not need to be near the bottom as that will not affect your trim enough to make a difference.

The only time you want the bands/clamps farther down on the cylinders is if placing them even with the attachment point allows the bottom of the cylinders to drop down. That would be like setting up a teeter-totter or see-saw with the pivot point closer to one end. If the support of the teeter-totter isn't in the center, the longer end will stay on the ground with the shorter end in the air. The same thing happens with long cylinders. If the band/clamp is not centered along the weight distribution of the cylinder (keeping in mind the valve and 1st stage add weight to that end), the heavier end will be lower. We want the valve end to be slightly heavier because we are supporting it with bungee to keep it in the armpits. If the opposite end is heavier, it will affect the pivot on the leash and drop down causing the valves to push up above your shoulders. In this case, the bands/clamps should be lowered to allow the valve end to be slightly heavier, keeping them in your armpits and allowing the cylinders to hang horizontally in the water.

You also want to place hose retainers or innertube on the cylinders. You will need two hose retainers on

Off set teeter-totter causes the longer end to be heavier and drop lower.

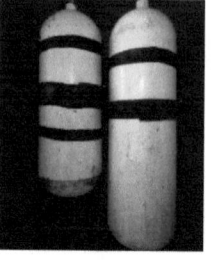

LP 95 cf/15 L and LP 120 cf/20 L cylinders. Note the band on the LP 120/20 L cylinder is lower.

Innertube on sidemount cylinders

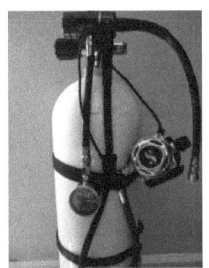

Short hose regulator secured to cylinder with hose retainer

any cylinder where you use a long hose to store the excess length. You may want one hose retainer on any cylinder with a short hose. The purpose of the hose retainers on the cylinders with short hoses is to hold the hose in place as you transport the cylinder to the water so it doesn't drag on the ground. If you're diving from a boat and placing the cylinders in the water before clipping them on, it will provide a place to stow the hose. It's also helpful to use innertube around the cam bands or clamps. With cam bands, the innertube helps keep the band secured to itself and prevents fishing line from getting caught between the Velcro on the straps. With worm gear clamps, the innertube covers the metal and helps protect your gear and the environment you're diving in.

Another use for the innertube is a backup fin strap. Several years ago, I was moving through a restriction that required me to push one of my cylinders ahead of me and lost one of my fins. When I reached a point where I could turn around, I went back through zero visibility feeling for the fin. I found it, but the strap had come off. I continued to search for the strap, in zero visibility, with one cylinder pushed in front of me and holding onto a fin. I didn't find the strap. As I was exiting the restriction for the second time, I thought about having to swim out from where I was, more than 2000 feet/600 meters from the entrance, with only one fin. As the visibility started to clear up, I noticed the innertube on the cylinder I was pushing in front of me that was used to secure the short hose. Once I was back into decent size passage, I removed the innertube before reclipping the cylinder. I then put my fin on and wrapped the innertube over the strap attachment points and around my heel. The innertube held in place the entire swim out. I was able to swim normally and exit without delay. You may not experience a similar situation, but you could potentially salvage a dive you're on if you break or lose a fin strap. All you'll need is the innertube from your cylinder.

Now that we have the sidemount rig and cylinders set up, let's jump in the water and fine tune things. This is where a good buddy and a camera will be useful.

10 ACHIEVING PROPER TRIM IN SIDEMOUNT
GETTING WET

Now that your rig is properly adjusted, it's time to get in the water and trim the cylinders. Don't try sidemount for the first time from a boat! You will have lots of difficulty with it and hold up the other divers. Even if it's your own boat, trying to get everything situated the first time while floating in the water will not be easy. Find a pool or an easy, shallow, open water shore entry that you're familiar with.

Once you have your cylinders at or in the water, get suited up, put on your rig, get in the water, and prepare to put your cylinders on. If you have somewhere in the water to set your cylinders so they won't get lost, set them there. If not, then clip them onto your chest D-rings if you are using neck clips or to your rear attachment points if you only have lower bolt snaps on your cylinders. Now that your hands are free, start by putting on your fins. It's often easier to get your fins on before your cylinders.

If you chose the short hose and long hose configuration and routed the hoses around your neck, it's recommended that you put the cylinder with the short hose on before the other one. By attaching that cylinder first, you will avoid trapping the long hose under the short hose. Other than the issue of trapping a hose, it doesn't matter which order you go with, but consistency helps promote efficiency, so choose one way and follow it. Start building your routine now so that it's always the same.

If you are using a leashed bolt snap around the neck, clip it to a chest D-ring on the side the cylinder will be positioned. This bolt snap holds the cylinder in place and allows both hands to be free while donning the cylinders. If you have two D-rings on each shoulder strap, it usually works better to clip onto the bottom one. If you stow your dive lights on your shoulder straps, make sure you clip the cylinder neck bolt snap to the outside of the dive light bolt snap so the dive light bolt snap isn't trapped under the leash. This makes deployment of the dive light easier should you need it. If you orient your cylinders with the 1st stages in your armpits and you are using a long hose on this cylinder, make sure the 2nd stage is positioned in front of the cylinder and your torso. This will prevent the 2nd stage from becoming trapped behind the cylinder, making it nearly impossible to pull it out and place it in position. There are a lot of ifs and whys here. There is no established method of sidemount and likely never will be. People dive sidemount for a variety of reasons, and this allows for a variety of configurations.

Next clip the lower bolt snap or carabiner (depending on which method you chose to use) to the butt plate or rear waist D-ring. This keeps the cylinder secured to your rig while you route the hoses. There are some rigs and body types in which reversing these steps may facilitate the process. With rigs that use narrow butt plates, clipping to the rails first will be easier. If you clip onto a chest D-ring and have difficulty clipping to the rear attachment point, try reversing the steps and clipping onto the rear first and then the chest. If that works better for you, then keep doing it that way!

2nd stage must be pulled in front of the cylinder so it can be easily pulled up. If you forget to do this step, you may have to unclip the cylinder to get the 2nd stage to the front.

If you do not use a clip around the neck, then you'll need to bungee the valve at this point to hold the cylinders in place. This option is acceptable, but it can make it a little difficult to route and attach inflator hoses and regulator hoses. But again, do what works for you. Just be aware of the options available.

Once the cylinders are secured in place, attach the low pressure inflator hose to your power inflator or your dry suit inflator. Where it gets hooked up depends on what side your power inflator comes off of and which cylinder you put on first. Let's assume you're going to connect it to the power inflator. If you have the power inflator coming off the top of your wing, you can route the hose over your shoulder and down alongside the corrugated inflator hose into the power inflator. If your inflator comes off of the bottom of the wing, route the hose under the shoulder strap, then up over the chest strap (if you have one) onto the power inflator. Make sure the inflator hose is long enough to allow you to orally inflate your wing. Don't forget the discussion in chapter 4 about inflator hose length. Shorter hoses have shorter life times because of the tension that is placed on the o ring. They also place stress on the power inflator. A few extra inches can extend the life of your hose significantly and save your power inflator from breaking.

Now pull the 2nd stage regulator up and either clip it to a D-ring or route the hose around your neck and clip it or place the necklace bungee over your head. If you are using neck leashes, move onto the next cylinder. You will secure the valve in the bungee after both cylinders are in place.

Inflator hose routes under the shoulder strap and onto the power inflator

Take the second cylinder and clip it to your rig in the same manner as the first one. If you are wearing a dry suit, route the low pressure hose under the shoulder strap below the chest strap (if you use one), and then feed it over the chest strap and connect it to your dry suit inflator. Pull the 2nd stage up to your D-ring or around your neck.

Now that both cylinders are in place with hoses routed, it's time to bungee the cylinder valves. If you are using ring bungees, routing the bungees around the neck, or routing loop bungees inside the valve to reverse the rotation, you will have to clip each cylinder on individually because you'll need both hands to do each one. If you are using loop or standard bungees around the outside of the valves, it may be easier to pull them over the valves at the same time. If you pull one side over the valve, this can shift the rig to that side and make the other side a little more difficult to bungee onto the valve.

Once the bungees are in place, you're ready to do your pre-dive check and go diving. Descend, get neutral, and pull the cylinders toward your head so they are in your armpits. This is an important step in the process. When you're standing up or floating vertically on the surface, gravity causes the cylinders to hang down from your rig. When you drop underwater and get horizontal, the cylinders will settle into place, but they will most likely not be far enough forward. So grab the valves, pull them forward, and let them settle into place in your armpits. If your sidemount rig has a butt plate with rails, you want those lower bolt snaps to be positioned at the top of the rails as discussed in chapter 8.

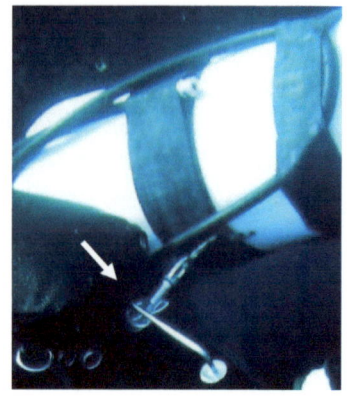

Bolt snap locked in place at the top of the rail

Now relax. Get into a proper horizontal position and allow your body to settle whichever way it does. This may mean you end up head down or feet down, or listing to one side or the other. In a properly adjusted sidemount rig, you should be horizontal without listing and no effort. If that isn't happening, adjustments need to be made. But you need to know what's happening in order to correct it.

Have someone look at your orientation in the water. Photographs are invaluable at this point so that you can see what you look like. But you must make sure the photographs are taken while you are motionless. Do not swim around or fin to hold position. That will not allow a true evaluation. You need to be completely motionless and allow your body to do whatever is natural, even if that means your head is on the bottom and your feet are above you! Based on what is happening, you may have to make adjustments to the length of the bungees, position of the bands/clamps, length of the cords on the bottom clips, and any other number of changes. This is where an experienced sidemount diver as a mentor or instructor can really help.

This diver is far too head heavy or foot light. He could counteract this by finning but then we would never know the problem exists and that it has to be fixed.

The first thing you want to adjust is the cylinders to your body. The cylinders should be in line with your body and on the same plane. Ideally, you want the front of the cylinders on the same plane as the front of your body. The first thing you need to evaluate is where the front of the band/clamp is in relation to the front of your body. If it's too low, then you need to shorten the leash or move the rear D-ring closer to your spine. If it sits higher than the front of your body, then you need to lengthen the leashes or move the D-ring forward.

The front of the cylinder is in line with the front of the body.

The front of the cam band is in the correct location, but the valve is positioned too low causing the bottom of the cylinder to rise up.

Make one adjustment at a time. Make that adjustment and evaluate. Make another adjustment and evaluate. Making too many adjustments at once may make things worse because each adjustment affects others. You could end up counteracting one adjustment with another. Get the cylinders lined up with your body before moving to the next adjustment.

Once you have the front of the bands/clamps where they should be, take a look at the valves. The valves should be nestled in your armpits. Typically, the valves will be too low and you'll need to shorten the valve bungees. When the bungees are too long and the valves too low, that will cause the bottoms of the cylinders to angle up and be too high. When you adjust the valve bungees and pull the valves up into your armpits, the bottoms of the cylinders will swing down. Remember that teeter-totter example in the last chapter? Same concept here. This is why you make one adjustment at a time. If you shortened the bungees and lengthened the leashes, the cylinders would hang too low.

When you're done with this adjustment, the cylinders should be in line with your body. The next thing to evaluate is your trim in the water.

Are you horizontal? Or are you heavy on one end or the other? New sidemount divers tend to be foot heavy. This is because the mass of the weight has been moved lower on the body where there isn't as much mass. With cylinders on your back, the main mass of the cylinders is placed between your waist and your shoulders, which is where the majority of the mass on your body is located. When you move the cylinders down below the shoulders, the majority of the cylinders is below your lungs, and the second heaviest part of the cylinder is below your waist and next to your thighs. Your feet are mainly bones, muscle, and skin. There's not much there that's buoyant, yet they have to counteract the buoyancy of the air in your lungs.

So how do you address the issue of heavy feet? First, you need to evaluate what is causing the heavy feet. Is it for the reasons just described? Or is it being caused by the design of your sidemount rig? If it's the reason just described, the solution may be a little easier.

Manufacturers have tried to address this issue for a long time by creating sidemount wings with more air space at the lower end of the wing. You see this in the design of horseshoe and donut shaped wings. Bungees were also used to trap air in the lower part of the wing. Smaller rigs, like those made for aluminum cylinders, tend to have the wings positioned over the lower back, so when inflated the lift is closer to the feet. One manufacturer even introduced a wing designed to fit under the butt plate and create more lift closer to the feet. The main issue with this was that it created an additional task for divers to deal with when changing depth. So in addition to releasing air from the main wing, they had to remember to also release air from the trim wing.

Another option that has been used for some years is the placement of trim weights on the shoulder webbing of the harness. By placing weights on the opposite end, the heaviness of the feet is counteracted and trim is corrected so the body is in a horizontal position. The weights can be placed on the front of the rig over the chest or on the back just above the shoulders.

Before continuing with this topic, I want to address ditchable weights. Many recreational open water divers believe they are absolutely necessary. Many years ago, when I was a member of a search and recovery team, I was told I had to have ditchable weights on my rig when they noticed I didn't have any. They were adamant about this until

Shoulder weight threaded on webbing under chest D-ring in the top photo & positioned above chest D-ring using bungee in the bottom photo

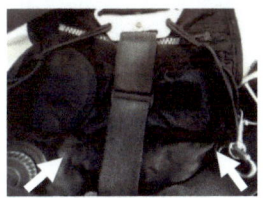

Weight pockets located on the inside of the wing near the top also act as trim weights

I explained that I didn't have any additional weight on my rig to ditch. That appeased them, but only to a degree. They didn't want to accept the concept of not having ditchable weights. I understood. After all, it's what we're taught in our basic open water classes.

Once you cross over into the world of technical diving, ditchable weights are no longer used. Instead, we adjust our rigs until they are balanced, and we make sure that we either have a backup buoyancy device or we can swim to the surface. If you want ditchable weight, be all means, use them. You just may need to get creative in how you place them on your rig because sidemount rigs do not come with that concept in mind.

If you place the weights in the chest area, you can thread the shoulder strap webbing through the weight and position it just above the chest D-ring or with the D-ring centered over the weight. If you travel with your rig, taking a weighted rig isn't practical. You can secure the weights to the webbing using bungee. This allows easy removal of the weights, as well as giving you the option of having ditchable weights. All you need is a cutting tool to cut the bungee. Bring the bungee with you and secure rental weights at your destination.

To secure weights using bungee, cut about 16 inches/40 cm of bungee and tie the ends together. Feed the loop end down through one of the slots from the front of the weight. Place the weight on the webbing and feed the loop under the webbing and back up through the other slot. Wrap the loop over the other side of the weight. Pull the knotted side and wrap that around the opposite side. You now have a weight secured onto your harness. (See

Appendix A for these instructions along with photos of each step.)

Manufacturers have added weight pockets positioned at the tops of the wings as well as weight pockets along the spine of the harness. Some of the smaller pillow shaped wings have pockets built in at the top, either one at the center or one on each side of the wing. You can also add weight pockets yourself or purchase spine pockets specifically designed for sidemount that you can add to your harness. I don't recommend weight pockets on the front of the harness as they will hang too low.

Which method of trimming out is correct? Well, that depends. If you are already overweighted, then adding more weight is not a good idea. Remember that neutral buoyancy test we all learned in our open water class? The first thing to do is get in the water with your sidemount system and cylinders that are nearly empty. Do a neutral buoyancy test by floating at the surface, taking in a normal breath, and holding it. If you are neutrally buoyant, you will drop to eye level with the surface. Once you exhale that normal breath, you should descend below the surface. If you don't descend, then you have to add weight.

Proper weighting does not mean being neutrally buoyant at the end of a normal dive. It means being neutrally buoyant at the end of a dive where you've had to tap into your emergency air reserves. That means you will be "overweighted" during all of your normal dives. But it's better to have that than to be too light when something goes wrong and causes you to have to breathe your cylinders empty. You don't want to be positively buoyant while trying to hold a safety stop at 15 feet/4.5 m.

Weight pockets along inside spine of sidemount harness when all that is needed is weight along center mass

Many divers will need additional weight, especially if you use a dry suit. However, if you're one of those that does not need additional weight, then adding trim weight is not an option. If you are neutrally buoyant with empty cylinders, the best option is to try to configure your rig so your body position is horizontal. If you're still overweighted with empty cylinders, using the wing to maintain that horizontal position may work for you. However, if you are neutral with empty cylinders, that means you won't have any air in your wing at that point so you won't be able to shift air to compensate for a foot heavy position. This is something that needs to be considered. If you're using air in your wing to raise your feet so you're horizontal, then what happens when your cylinders get lighter as you breathe them down and you no longer need as much air in your wing? You'll end up losing that horizontal trim as well.

If you can't get horizontal no matter what adjustments you make, you'll need to consider using different cylinders. You might need shorter or smaller, lighter cylinders. That might mean less air, but you'll make up for that with a lower air consumption rate by not struggling as much with cylinders that don't allow you to get horizontally trimmed.

If you do need additional weight, why not have that weight serve two purposes? Use it as neutral buoyancy and trim weight. Why use trim weight rather than shifting air lower in the wing to correct trim? Well, first off, as stated above, when neutral, you won't have any air in your wing. Second, trim weight won't fail, but wings do fail. I have personally had three wing failures and know several other divers who have had wing failures as well. If you depend on having air in your wing to maintain proper horizontal trim, then should you have a wing failure, you will also have trim failure. If a wing failure causes you to go from having near perfect horizontal trim to having a 25-30 degree angle or more to your body, you will not only be dealing with poor trim, but you will also be creating significant drag with the larger profile. This will in turn increase your air consumption. If you have to swim back to the dive boat because it's unsafe to surface directly overhead, it will take a lot longer than it should.

Most of us who use steel cylinders also have redundant buoyancy control. For many, that redundancy is in the form of a dry suit. If you wear a wetsuit while using steel cylinders, you probably have a second wing bladder. If you don't, you should consider it. With a wing failure, we automatically go to our redundant buoyancy. It's what we're taught. If you're also depending on your wing for trim, you'll need to depend on your dry suit for trim as well. This isn't as easy as with a wing and also requires having to put more air at the feet, something which many of us try to avoid. If you have a redundant bladder, it's usually not as large and won't provide as much lift as the primary bladder. This means it will not help you out much with your trim. Bottom line is that you must choose the method that works best for you. If you need to add weight anyway, then ask yourself, "What are you weighting for?"

Diver suffering from Knee Drop Syndrome (KDS). The cylinders are horizontal but the knees are being forced to drop below them as the bottoms are raised up by the wing.

There is another possible reason for heavy feet – rig design. Sidemount rigs that are designed with donut shaped wings routed underneath the butt plate can have a significant effect on trim. As we discussed in chapter 2, they raise the butt plate when they are inflated. I've mentioned that you are heavier at the beginning of the dive because of the air in your cylinders. As you breathe that air, you get lighter and don't need your wing to be as inflated. The cylinders are held in position by the bolt snap and leash located lower on the body. If they are not attached to a fixed point on your rig, the trim of the cylinders will change. This is what happens with donut shaped wings with the butt plate positioned above the wing.

This can cause your feet to feel heavy when you inflate the wing and the cylinders are raised up by the butt plate raising up. This is what is referred to as knee drop syndrome, or KDS. This happens with heavier steel cylinders. Because the cylinders make up a concentrated mass of weight on you as a diving unit, they tend to trim horizontally and force your body into a position in which your knees are dropped **more** than the rest of your body. As your cylinders get lighter from being breathed from, you require less air in your wing. This results in the butt plate getting closer to

2 inch/5 cm webbing across the center to hold weight. The center weight is secured in place using the bungee method described earlier.

your buttocks, thus dropping the bottom of the cylinders in relation to your body. In turn, your knees are not forced into as much of a drop as previously. They get closer to being in line with the cylinders. Depending on how you have your cylinders rigged, you might come to a point in your dive in which the cylinders are parallel to your body. Eventually, the cylinders may fall lower than your body. This is because the trim of the cylinders is dependent on the amount of air in the wing.

Let's get back to the discussion of weights for buoyancy. Where do you place additional weight that you may need but aren't also using as trim weight? With the foot heaviness issue, you don't want to place it on the waist because that will make you more foot heavy. There are a few options available.

As already mentioned, some sidemount rigs have weight pockets built into their design. Usually, these are positioned along the spine of the rig so that the weight can be placed center mass and not affect trim. If you don't have one of these rigs, you may need to improvise. There is a soft weight plate on the market that has several weight pockets and can be attached to the back of a rig on horseshoe and donut shaped wings using sex bolts. If your rig doesn't allow for this attachment, you should be able to add 2 inch/5 cm webbing across the center of the back that will hold additional weights. You can also check out some free diving weight vests. They work great for holding weights in place over the mid to upper back and can be worn under the sidemount rig.

Getting properly trimmed in sidemount is not easy for someone who hasn't done it before. A good mentor or instructor should be able to get someone new to sidemount diving trimmed properly in a matter of minutes if the gear is customized and the cylinders are pair matched. Doing it by yourself is going to be difficult because you need to be able to evaluate the changes you have made by looking at them. Feel is not enough. Don't give up. If it's just you and a buddy and neither of you have much, if any, sidemount experience, keep at it using the tips offered in this chapter.

11 BASIC SKILLS IN SIDEMOUNT

There are several basic skills when it comes to diving in sidemount. Many of them are no different than in any other configuration. However, some of them are specific to sidemount diving, or more in general, diving independent cylinders. This chapter focuses on the skills necessary in the water, but it does not substitute for the time in the water with a qualified mentor or instructor. You need to get in the water and practice the skills correctly so you can build the muscle memory to make these skills second nature.

The first thing you want to do in your new rig is learn the location of everything. This doesn't mean sit on your couch in your house with the lights out while learning where the D-rings, cutting tools, dive lights, etc., are located. First, you can't feel your rear pouch if you're sitting on it. But most importantly, the rig does not settle on your body sitting up on your couch the same way it will settle when you're in the water in a horizontal position with two cylinders putting tension on it. Remember the first thing you're supposed to do when you get in the water? Pull those cylinders into your armpits. So get out there and dive! There's no substitution for that.

Make sure you do it safely. Shallow fresh water is the best place to work on buoyancy and trim. You have a lot of time in the water and buoyancy changes are much more pronounced. Bring along a buddy as a spotter and to get photos or video.

You should spend time just learning where everything is located on your new sidemount rig. Once you have your trim worked out, you need to swim around and get comfortable with the new configuration. Choose somewhere to swim around in a big circle. This might get boring, but you need to get used to the new gear and learn where everything is located.

You may notice your legs hitting the bottoms of your sidemount cylinders as you're finning. This will feel strange, but it should tell you something. You are finning with your thighs rather than with your calves and feet. You can do a much more efficient and powerful fin stroke by finning with your calves, ankles, and feet. Keep the knees a few inches/centimeters apart and twist your ankles and feet to move the water behind you. Your air consumption rate will decrease because you're using smaller muscles, and you will reduce your drag by reducing the amount of movement you make. You'll find that you actually have a more powerful and efficient fin kick.

Getting in the water is the best thing you can do to build experience!

The most important things to build muscle memory with are your inflator and deflator. You shouldn't waste time looking for those when you need them. A slow descent or ascent can quickly turn into a fast one. When you reach for the inflator or deflator, your hand should go directly to it. This doesn't mean you need to inflate or exhaust air every time you reach for it. Grab the power inflator and find the button as if you are about to engage it. Grab the cord on the exhaust valve, but don't pull it. Don't just practice with one hand, either. Build the muscle memory with both hands! When you need to add air to your wing or release air from it, you need to do it quickly.

Practice deploying your lights and accessing your thigh pocket or rear pouch. Switch 2nd stage regulators often so you get used to that. Test yourself to see if you know which regulator you're breathing from a few minutes after a switch. I had my students switch every 100 psi/10 Bar the first couple of dives and would signal them out of air shortly after the switch to test their awareness. Constant practice is what it takes to build that muscle memory. As you start to get comfortable with knowing where everything is on your rig, you need to pay closer attention to air management.

An important skill to learn in sidemount that is an absolute necessity is proper air management. First, you need to stay within the limits of your training. You need to plan your dives according to your limits and plan your air usage. Because you are diving independent cylinders, you also need to manage the air between the cylinders. This means switching regulators on a regular basis to balance the air in them. And whatever air limits you are held to, sixths, thirds, back on the boat with 500 psi, or some other limit, you need to adhere to them in both cylinders.

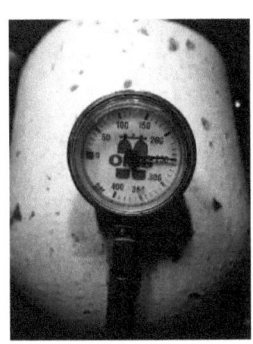

Keep your pressures within 600 psi/40 Bar of each other.

Some people will tell you that balancing the cylinders is important so that you stay balanced in the water. While it's true that having a large enough difference in pressure between the cylinders can cause you to list to one side, this does not happen all the time or with all cylinders. Some divers will breathe one cylinder all the way from 3000 psi/200 Bar to 2000 psi/140 Bar before switching to the other cylinder without affecting trim. Some will breathe an aluminum 80 cf/11 L cylinder from 3000 psi/200 Bar to 500 psi/35 Bar before switching to the other cylinder, and again there is no effect on trim. I dive a sidemounted single aluminum 80 cf/11 L cylinder in tropical locations regularly with no counterweight and am able to balance without effort. The issue with breathing one cylinder down so far before switching to the other is a matter of managing your emergency reserves. You need to have sufficient air in both cylinders should you need to air share with someone.

Let's look at a common air management exercise on a wreck dive. Diver A is diving aluminum 80 cf/11 L cylinders filled to 3000 psi/200 Bar. He plans on breathing his right cylinder, which has a long hose on it, from 3000 psi/200 Bar to 2000 psi/140 Bar When the pressure reaches 2100 psi/145 Bar, Diver A's buddy, Diver B, who is diving backmount, has a catastrophic air loss and has to share air. Diver A donates the long hose attached to the cylinder with only 2100 psi/145 Bar in it and switches to the left cylinder, which still has 2900 psi/190 Bar in it (100 psi/10 Bar has been used for wing inflation), and the team begins swimming to the anchor line, which happens to be on the opposite end of the wreck. Diver B's air consumption has increased because of the incident and remains elevated throughout the swim.

Even though only 900 psi/65 Bar of one cylinder has been used during penetration (under the assumption both divers have the same air consumption rate), Diver B uses 2000 psi/140 Bar to swim to the anchor line and ascend, leaving only 100 psi/10 Bar in that cylinder (it's not uncommon for air consumption to double or more in emergency situations). While this still gets both divers out alive, it's pretty close and doesn't leave room for any other emergencies.

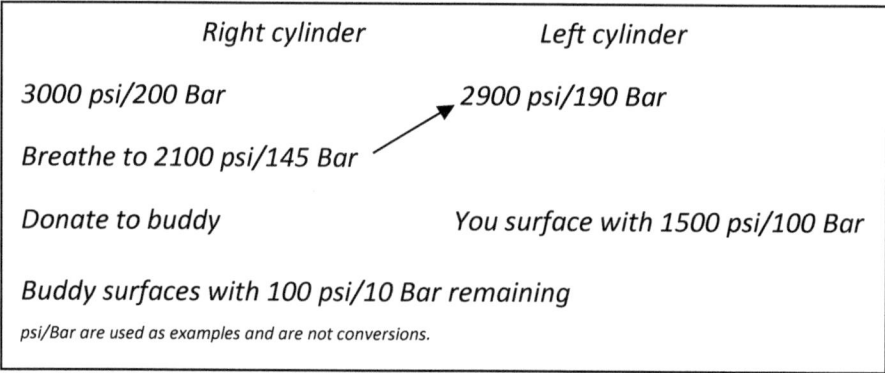

Right cylinder	Left cylinder
3000 psi/200 Bar	2900 psi/190 Bar
Breathe to 2100 psi/145 Bar	
Donate to buddy	You surface with 1500 psi/100 Bar
Buddy surfaces with 100 psi/10 Bar remaining	

psi/Bar are used as examples and are not conversions.

In the same situation, if Diver A had managed air between cylinders by switching regulators every 500 psi/35 Bar, Diver B would have 500 psi/35 Bar left in that cylinder. Diver A would have switched at 2500 psi/170 Bar, breathed the other cylinder to 2500 psi/170 Bar before the incident happened, and donated a regulator attached to a cylinder with 2500 psi/170 Bar still in it. Diver A would have the same amount of air in both cylinders at the time of the incident. Diver B's increased air consumption would still have gotten him out with less air than Diver A, but he would have had a buffer of 500 psi/35 Bar versus only 100 psi/10 Bar. Given the inaccuracy of most SPGs and the possibility of breathing at a higher rate, a larger buffer is always better.

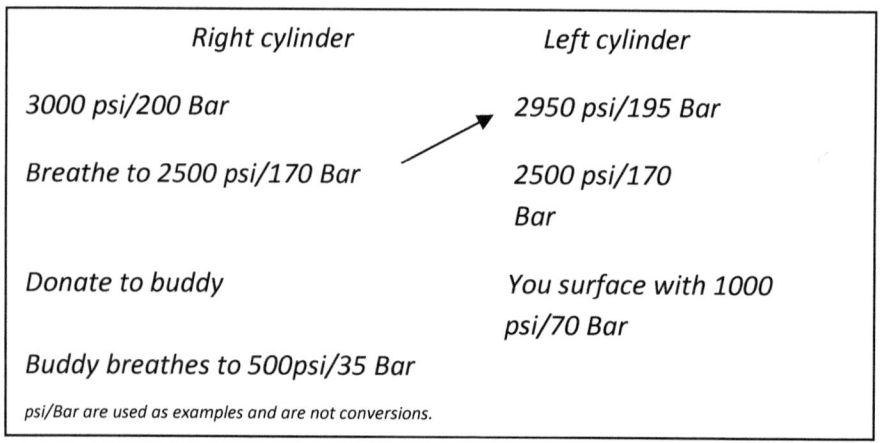

Right cylinder	Left cylinder
3000 psi/200 Bar	2950 psi/195 Bar
Breathe to 2500 psi/170 Bar	2500 psi/170 Bar
Donate to buddy	You surface with 1000 psi/70 Bar
Buddy breathes to 500psi/35 Bar	

psi/Bar are used as examples and are not conversions.

 While there's no guarantee that an incident will occur when the cylinder pressures are balanced, switching regulators every 400-600 psi/25-40 Bar will ensure that the pressures will remain close enough in an emergency.

What's the likelihood of this happening? In all honesty, there's not a great chance of such an incident occurring. These days, equipment is better quality, divers watch their air pressure closely, and with independent cylinders, having to share air is not very likely. However, as divers we must always plan for the worst case scenarios, and switching regulators every 500 psi/35 Bar does not add much more work to the dive. Switching every 1000 psi/70 Bar involves two regulator switches – breathe the right cylinder to 2000 psi/140 Bar, switch, breathe the left cylinder to 1000 psi/70 Bar, switch, breathe the right cylinder to 500 psi/70 Bar, switch, breathe the left cylinder to 500 psi/35 Bar, switch, and end the dive.

Doing regulator switches every 500 psi/35 Bar involves one additional regulator switch – breathe right cylinder to 2500 psi/165 Bar, switch, breathe left cylinder to 2000 psi/140 Bar, switch, breathe right cylinder to 1500 psi/105 Bar, switch, breathe the left cylinder to 500 psi/35 Bar, switch, end the dive after breathing the right cylinder to 500 psi/35 Bar. One additional regulator switch is a very small price to pay for the added security of having the air in both cylinders more closely matched.

An additional reason for balancing the cylinders more frequently is to ensure your regulators are in working condition. This is something that's not done often enough in recreational scuba diving. When was the last time you tested your octopus regulator? Does it breathe well? Does it breathe dry? Breathing from both regulators more often in sidemount ensures that both are working properly and ready to be used when needed.

Another key skill in diving sidemount is the air share. Unless you have chosen to use two long hoses in your configuration, you will always have to donate a particular regulator. During half of the dive, that regulator will not be in your mouth, but clipped off to your D-ring or in a necklace bungee. It is extremely important to know which regulator needs to be donated. An easy way to help you with this is to use two different mouthpieces on your regulators. By doing this, you will be able to tell which regulator you are breathing from simply by the feel of the mouthpiece in your mouth. Another option, if you're like me and have a preference for a particular type of mouthpiece, is to snip off a small piece of one mouthpiece so you can feel the difference with your tongue. It doesn't take much to be able to feel this. You will have to build the muscle memory of feeling for that difference and making sure you're aware of which cylinder you're breathing from. I typically do this to the mouthpiece on the 2nd stage that I will not be donating, so if I have to donate, the recipient is getting a standard mouthpiece. Although the bit I snip off is almost not noticeable if you aren't aware of the minor modification.

Mouthpiece on right has the edge of the left inner piece snipped off. This is easily felt with the tongue.

Ziplock bag with small zip ties to secure bolt snap onto 2nd stage regulator

Also, as mentioned in chapter 5, you should use a zip tie, o-ring, bungee, or one of the commercially manufactured clip holders to secure the bolt snap to your long hose regulator. However, if you only practice deploying that regulator by unclipping the bolt snap from the D-ring, that is the muscle memory you will build. Practice breaking away the regulator. Zip ties and o-rings are inexpensive and easy to replace. Remember to carry a small bag with zip ties in it so you can replace the broken one and have somewhere to put it. Use them to build that muscle memory and get comfortable with this skill.

Once the air management and air sharing skills have been mastered, the next skill to begin working on is removing items from thigh pockets. This seems to present a problem to many new sidemount divers, yet it's a simple task if approached the proper way. Because the cylinders are positioned over the thigh pockets, the pockets cannot be accessed the same way as in backmount. Many new sidemount divers make the mistake of trying to access pockets from above the cylinders. The cylinders are too close to the thigh and cannot be moved out enough

Accessing thigh pocket by pushing sidemount cylinder up and out of the way to expose the pocket so it can be reached

for this to be practical. The cylinders need to be moved out of the way and the pockets accessed from below.

With your upper arm and elbow, push the cylinder up and away from your side so it rests on your flank. Once the cylinder is out of the way, you can access pocket contents much more easily. Reach into the pocket and remove whatever you need. Close the pocket and let the cylinder drop back down to your side. Make sure to pull the valve up into your armpits in case it shifted position when you pushed it up.

Some dry suit manufacturers now offer a "sidemount" dry suit. This is a dry suit with the thigh pocket positioned on the front of the thigh, so it is not under the cylinder where it is more difficult to access. There are advantages and disadvantages to this. It does get the pocket out from under the cylinder. However, placing it under you, the pocket can snag on things below you if you're not used to needing the additional clearance. In that position, the pocket can also be more difficult to access because it can be harder to reach when located in the front that low.

Even knowing how to easily access pocket contents, some divers prefer not to use thigh pockets. Another option is to carry contents in a detached pouch that can be clipped to D-rings or the rails on the butt plate or a rear D-ring. By keeping contents in a removable pouch, the pouch can be held in front of you and viewed so contents can easily be retrieved and the pouch clipped back when contents are in hand. Some divers use both.

If you use a thigh pocket, you will need to consider what you place in it. If one pocket contains flat items like wetnotes, and the other pocket contains an SMB and a backup mask, the pocket with the bulkier items will prevent the cylinder on that side from hanging evenly with the other cylinder. You can either make sure the pockets are both equally sized with all contents, or you can lengthen the leash on the side of the larger bulge to account for that. This will allow the cylinder to sit a little farther out but on the same plane as the opposite one. Even if you end up with a thigh pocket located on the front, you may prefer to keep less bulky items in that pocket.

You can also choose to use thigh pockets for certain types of items and a rear pouch for other types of items. Personally, I prefer to keep items I will likely need during the dive in my thigh pocket where they are easily accessible and emergency items that I'm unlikely to need in my rear pouch. My wetnotes and line markers are stored in my thigh pockets (I end up doing survey on many of my cave dives and use my wetnotes for that). My backup mask, lights, and spools go into the rear pouch. This keeps flat items in the thigh pocket and bulkier items in the pouch. I clip my SMB to a rear D-ring rather than place it in a pocket.

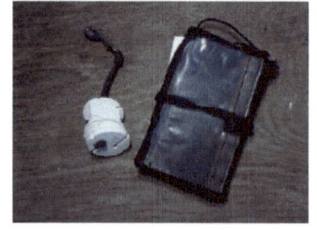

Typical pocket contents. Larger contents go into the rear pouch and smaller/flatter contents go in thigh pocket.

A final consideration when choosing pockets is how they remain closed. The options available are Velcro and zipper. Both do a good job of keeping the pocket closed and contents secure. The only difference I can think of between the two is how you open them. I can open a Velcro pocket with one hand quite easily. This is useful for thigh pockets that I am accessing with one hand. With a zipper closure, I may need both hands to get the zipper open. Velcro will last a long time even with lots of exposure to water. I've never had an issue with a pocket coming open unintentionally. I can even access a pouch with a Velcro closure clipped to a rear D-ring with one hand. That's a little more difficult to do with a zipper pouch.

Once you've decided where you want to store your gear, you need to practice retrieving it. Practice pushing your cylinder out of the way and getting your items from your thigh pocket. Remove the pouch from the rear D-ring and hold it in front of you. To challenge yourself, try removing something from a rear pouch with one hand without unclipping the pouch.

With our discussion of pockets and how to access them completed, it's time to turn to the items that we'll be carrying in them as well as other sidemount diving gear accessories.

Various pouches

12 SIDEMOUNT ACCESSORIES

You've achieved proper trim, you can don and doff your rig and cylinders efficiently, and you have your basic skills down. What's next? Accessories. As divers, we all love our toys. We continually look for new dive gear to buy and add to the kit. This isn't any different when it comes to sidemount. Your addiction may become worse. The main accessories we'll look at with sidemount are dive lights, pockets/pouches, and argon cylinders.

Dive lights

Let's start with the primary light. If you intend to keep using a small handheld dive light for your night dives, you can skip this section. If you are considering moving to a bigger and brighter dive light, read on.

Handheld 8000 lumen LED primary light. Compact and lightweight.

Not so long ago, the only option divers had for primary lights that were bright and had decent burn time were cabled lights. While not as popular among recreational scuba divers, there are some that use cabled dive lights for night diving. This is no longer necessary. You can cut the cord and get bright lights with decent burn time. We now have many options in handheld lights that are both bright (even brighter than most cabled lights) and can last 2-4 hours on a single charge. Because of this, many sidemount divers are opting to go with handheld cordless lights rather than the cabled canister lights.

More and more light manufacturers are offering primary lights with sufficient brightness and burn times to allow for smaller batteries and the elimination of a cable. The entire light is low enough in weight to be carried on the back of the hand without the need for a cable and separate battery canister mounted elsewhere on the body. Unlike just a few years ago, we no longer have to sacrifice brightness or burn time to achieve this. You can get 8000 lumens with a two hour burn time, which is sufficient for most divers, technical divers included. If you need more than that, add a spare battery to your kit and swap batteries during your surface interval. Or you can decrease your output to 4000 lumens and double the burn time.

There are a couple of advantages in doing away with the canister and cable. First, you don't have to try to find the best location and method to carry the canister. We'll discuss this in more detail. You also don't have to deal with trying to route a cable from your canister to the light head on your hand. Many divers will try to route the cable inside the harness to limit its exposure to the surroundings, but you will always have some of the cable exposed and presenting a possible snag hazard.

Maybe you want to continue to use the cabled light you already own, or maybe you prefer it over a handheld model. You will have to consider where to mount the battery canister so it is out of the way and doesn't interfere with anything else. There are a few options to mounting the battery canister. It can be mounted on the waist strap similar to how it's mounted with backmount configuration. It can be mounted across the lower back or across the upper thighs. Some divers even choose to mount it along the spine webbing of the harness under the wing.

The first option we'll discuss is mounting the battery canister on the right side of the waist as done traditionally in backmount. This works fine and allows for the use of the same light with no alterations needed in cable length or style. You can position the canister on your waist so that it sits in the area where your cylinder and torso meet. This should keep its profile even with the bottom plane of the cylinder.

One consideration is the size of the battery canister. If the canister has a large diameter, it might stick out a little, but this is usually not sufficient enough to make much of a difference. And with today's battery technology, we're getting smaller batteries with more power, so large canisters are a thing of the past. Smaller diameter canisters that are

Cabled canister lights must be mounted higher on the back due to the shorter cable.

Mounting at thighs is possible with a longer cable. Note the angled cable connection on the canister made specifically for sidemount.

shorter will be less obtrusive in this position than a wider canister that is 12 inches/30 cm long.

If you don't like the battery canister in this location, you can mount it on your back. To do this, you will need two small worm gear clamps, 20 inches/50 cm of static cord, and two bolt snaps. Cut the cord into two even pieces and tie them into loops. Loop the bolt snaps on one end. Then secure the knotted end to the canister body with the clamps.

Where you mount it behind you will be largely dictated by the length of the cable between the battery and the light head. Cable length on most standard canister lights is 40-44 inches/100-120 cm. For the average height diver, this means the battery canister must be mounted higher on the back of the rig so that there is enough cable length to mount the light head on the hand with the arm in a normal extended position. This can cause an issue if you plan to go through swim-throughs or into wrecks. Mounting the canister in this location places it so that it is over the buttocks or the lower back. While the lower back would be the better of the two options because the buttocks typically stick out more than the back, the battery canister will still create a higher profile in this position.

Another option is to order a light with a slightly longer cable, or send your light to the manufacturer to have a longer cable installed. A length of 50 inches/125 cm is usually sufficient. This allows the battery canister to be mounted on the butt plate or on offset D-rings so that it can hang just below the buttocks over the upper thighs. This is the lowest area behind you and holds it at a profile low enough to not pose any issues. Some divers bungee the canister under the crotch strap so that it is held tightly against the legs. The canister can be pulled out of the bungee if needed, but replacing it is more difficult than just having to reclip it. This also prevents you from being able to keep the crotch strap snug.

Manufacturers also have an angled cable connection for canister lights used in sidemount. The cable comes off of the canister at a right angle to minimize the loop that is formed by a cable coming straight out of the top of the canister. It also minimizes the amount of stress on that part of the cable.

A final option for mounting the battery canister is to secure it along the spine webbing of the harness under the wing. This gets the canister out of the way and allows you to route the cable under the wing and harness. There are a few disadvantages to this. First, you need to have a light with a power switch on the head as you won't be able to reach the canister under your wing. Second, as with mounting the canister at your lower back, it creates a higher profile. This isn't that big of a deal for recreational scuba divers.

Another disadvantage, and this is the more important one, is that mounting the canister in this location will affect your trim. The canister positioned under the wing prevents that side of the wing from being able to inflate as much as the opposite side. So when you have air in your wing, more air will be on the opposite side, and this can cause you to list to the side of the canister. You may be able to minimize this with smaller canisters, but larger canisters will definitely cause a problem.

Battery canister mounted left of the spine. This position affects the way the wing inflates and could result in listing to the left because it prevents that side from fully inflating, forcing more air to settle in the opposite side of the wing. This creates less lift on the side of the canister and more lift on the opposite side in addition to having the weight of the canister on the left.

Mask mounted light. Power button rather than light head rotation allows activation with one hand.

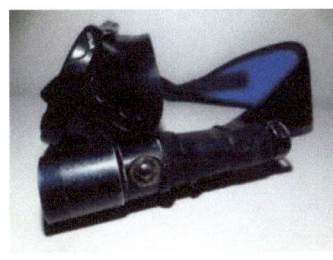

Bicycle innertube is used to mount light to mask strap. The light must be compact and lightweight enough so it doesn't affect how the mask rests on your face and doesn't put undue stress on the mask strap.

Another light option popular with sidemount divers is mask and helmet mounted lights. Small, lightweight dive lights are being mounted on one or both sides of the mask onto the strap. These lights are mainly being used as backup lights or to use on occasion throughout the dive to illuminate things when your hands are occupied. They are not intended to be powered on constantly throughout the dive. The main advantage to this is being able to see gauges easily during night dives. If you orient your cylinders with the valve openings facing up and position your SPGs along the cylinders, they will be located above you. While you may be able reach them and pull them into view, illuminating the face of the gauges will not be as easy. Having a light on your mask allows you to pull the gauge out far enough to see and illuminate at the same time just by turning your head toward it. If you use transmitters, then this isn't applicable. If you use a mask light in the event of a primary dive light failure, be prepared to remove it from the mask. Signaling with a mask light is not ideal. You could end up with whiplash!

The easiest way to mount lights to your mask is with a length of bicycle innertube slightly shorter than the light with the mask strap and light routed through it. A consideration when choosing a mask light is how it is powered on and off. While lights with twist on heads tend to be preferred by some, these lights require the use of both hands to activate. This is not always easy or practical for a mask light. Having a light with a power button that can be activated with one hand is preferred so the light can be turned on and off quickly.

Pockets/Pouches

Removable pockets/pouches are a very useful tool in sidemount. As discussed in chapter 11, thigh pockets can be used and are easily accessed. However, placing a lot of tools in a thigh pocket can cause cylinders to be out of trim. The alternative solution is to carry a pocket or pouch that can be clipped to the back of the sidemount rig and removed so the diver can look at it and access it directly in front. This makes it easier to retrieve tools in the pouch because you can actually see what you're getting. You can also use both hands to access the pouch. Just use your dive light or mask light to illuminate what you're seeing.

Zipper pouch

Pouches come in a variety of shapes and sizes. Some are thin and only meant to carry small items like wetnotes, pencils, cutting tools, other small tools, and small lights. Others can expand and allow you to carry masks and spools in them as well. Because it's mounted behind you and out of the way, it's easy to stuff it full of items, clip it off, and forget it's there. You don't want the pouch to be too bulky, but you also want it to be large enough to be useful. Check out the pouches available on the market.

Double enders clipped onto an after-market thigh pouch so it can be used as a rear pouch

Don't limit yourself to only the pouches that are marketed for sidemount. My preference is a thigh pocket with the thigh straps removed. It is about mid-size and rests on top of my legs out of the way without going above the upper plane of my body.

Rear mounted pouch sits out of the way just below the butt plate.

Another consideration when choosing a rear pouch is how it

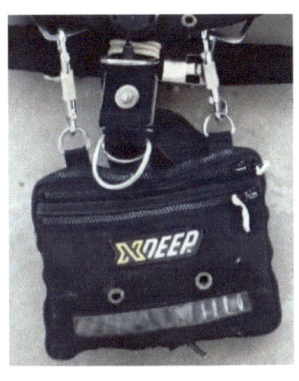

You can purchase a pocket specifically made for sidemount, such as the one pictured above, or one that isn't made for it (pictured below) but can be modified so it can be clipped somewhere behind you. The latter option will be much easier on your wallet.

closes. Pouches come with either zipper or Velcro closures. Zipper closures will stay closed, but they require both hands to open. Velcro closures allow you to open the pouch with one hand, something I've found useful when I need a tool I can easily identify by feel, like a spool or light. Velcro isn't as secure as a zipper, but if you inspect it regularly you will notice if it's starting to wear and needs to be replaced. I've had the bolt snap attachments on my pouches wear out long before the Velcro, and I've never had a Velcro pouch come open unintentionally.

Dry suit inflation cylinders

Dry suit inflation cylinders or argon cylinders are necessary for some divers. Whether you're diving colder waters and need the added warmth of the heavier gas or simply want a separate cylinder to use air to inflate your dry suit, you need to figure out where to put that additional cylinder. You have a couple of options for this.

One option is to hang it across your thighs from your butt plate or waist D-rings similar to the way a battery canister is carried. You will need two worm gear clamps, two bolt snaps, and 3 feet/1 meter of static line. Cut the line in half and fold over each section. Tie the loose ends into a knot and loop the bolt snaps onto the folded end. Position the clamps about 3 inches/8 cm from either end of the cylinder with the knotted end of the static cord under the clamp and tighten the clamps. The cylinder is now ready to hang from your waist or butt plate. When choosing a hose, you will need a slightly longer one to reach the dry suit inflator. Before taking this on a dive, make sure to get in the water and check your trim. The weight of the cylinder and 1st stage can cause you to become foot heavy and might need to be compensated for.

Another option is to mount the dry suit inflation cylinder above one of your sidemount cylinders in the crevice between the cylinder and your torso. It will nestle into that space and not be noticeable. The cylinder should be positioned with the bottom near the shoulder and the valve near the waist. You will need one worm gear clamp, 2 feet/60 cm of bungee, and two bolt snaps. Cut 1.5 feet/40 cm of the bungee. Fold the shorter length of bungee and tie the ends together into a knot. Loop the folded end around the bolt snap. Place the small loop around the neck of the cylinder. Fold and tie the long length of bungee in the same fashion, add a bolt snap, and attach this to the bottom end of the cylinder with the clamp. Clock the bungee so it is even with the valve opening. This will protect the 1st stage and position the handwheel so you can reach it with your left hand when mounted on the left. Clip the bolt snap on the longer bungee to a chest D-ring, routing the bungee under your arm, and clip the neck bolt snap to your butt plate rail or waist D-ring. Route the hose between your sidemount cylinder and hip, then up to the dry suit inflator.

Dry suit inflation cylinder is rigged to hang across thighs from butt plate or waist D-rings much like a cabled canister.

Dry suit inflation cylinder is rigged to top mount along the sidemount cylinder short bungee, bolt snap clipped onto butt plate rail or waist D-ring and long bungee bolt snap clipped to chest D-ring.

These are the most popular accessories used in recreational sidemount. As you can see, there are lots of options available to you as a sidemount diver. What works best for you depends on the type of diving you do. If you don't have a lot of items to carry, then a rear pouch isn't necessary. If you don't dive with a dry suit, then an inflation cylinder isn't necessary. Evaluate your diving needs before you spend a lot of money on gear that's going to be sitting in a rubber tub in your storage room.

Diving the C-53 wreck in Cozumel, Mexico. Note the "accessory" clipped to the rear D-ring.

13 SIDEMOUNT AND REBREATHERS

Sidemount has gained quite a bit of popularity among rebreather divers in recent years. Rebreather diving has also become popular among recreational scuba divers. Because of this, I felt a chapter on sidemount and rebreathers was warranted for the recreational sidemount diving book.

In the past, bailout cylinders were carried in the same manner as traditional stage cylinders, hanging from D-rings positioned on the front of the harness. This created a larger profile and much unneeded drag when moving through the water. The growing popularity of sidemount diving has caused many rebreather divers to rethink the way they rig their bailout cylinders. There aren't any major differences to sidemounting cylinders whether in a sidemount configuration only or with a rebreather on one's back. Some sidemount divers are purchasing a sidemount rig, attaching their rebreathers to it, and rigging up their bailout cylinders in the more streamlined configuration of sidemount. This works well for many, as there are sidemount rigs suitable for backmount, whether with manifolded cylinders or a rebreather.

Bailout cylinder hanging below the diver

Maybe you've been using a particular rig with your rebreather and want to streamline your bailout cylinders. You can adapt your current rig so that the bailout cylinders can be sidemounted. This is a viable option since the wing can taco up around the rebreather without causing any issues as discussed in chapter 7. The only change is attaching the bailout cylinders so they are sidemounted rather than slinging them like stage cylinders. This can easily be done by clipping the cylinders to D-rings at the rear of the waist strap unless the rebreather and wing comes down too far to allow that. Then you can simply add a butt plate or offset d-rings to the rig to secure the bottoms of the cylinders. Add bungees under the shoulders to hold the valves in place, and you can secure the valves in the armpits. Bailout cylinders can then be rigged as sidemount cylinders rather than traditional stage cylinders.

Bailout cylinder not in line with the body of the diver

The one thing to keep in mind is that by changing the orientation of the bailout cylinders, you are placing more weight toward the feet. This may require reconfiguring the weight on your rig. The likelihood of this is not great. You've already been slinging your bailout and are simply moving the cylinders toward your feet a few inches/centimeters. However, if you decide to start sidemounting steel cylinders as bailout, this might be an issue that needs to be addressed.

Black aluminum bailout cylinder sidemounted with rebreather backmounted. The bottom of the cylinder is even with the knees.

Another subtopic of sidemount and rebreathers is sidemounting a rebreather. Divers have been modifying rebreathers into sidemount systems or building their own sidemount rebreathers for decades. Some have been successful. Some have not. The two obstacles they have encountered are counterlung placement and loop routing. Over the past several years, a few manufacturers have designed and built sidemount rebreathers that are efficient and work well with the configuration. These rebreathers used to be classified as advanced rebreathers, but divers are converting from open circuit directly to sidemount rebreathers. I believe anyone desiring to begin diving rebreathers should seek and receive training and build experience in a traditional backmounted rebreather before attempting to begin diving a sidemounted rebreather.

The reason for this is that most sidemounted rebreathers have design features that make them more difficult to manage and affect their work of breathing. The first sidemount rebreathers, and most of the ones that exist today, are built as a single cylinder that houses the counterlung, scrubber, and oxygen sensors. The loop hoses are attached to the head of the cylinder and route directly to the mouth. The issue with this design is in having a single counterlung that is positioned at your side next to your hip.

To understand more about this, let's discuss the principles behind counterlungs and their position on the diver. Traditional backmount rebreathers come with counterlungs in one of two positions. The counterlungs are placed over the lungs on the back or over the lungs on the chest. The reason for this is that the counterlungs need to be as close as possible to our own lungs to minimize work of breathing. The farther they are from the lungs, the more difficult it will be to breathe through the rebreather loop.

Work of breathing is already increased in rebreathers due to many factors. The gas must pass through the scrubber media, past the corrugations of the loop hoses, through more than one valve, and it must deal with the pressure differential created by the position of the counterlungs. You can minimize some of those factors by the way you pack the scrubber media and by using the shortest possible loop hoses. Those effects are minimal. The main thing you can control is where the counterlungs are positioned.

Rear mounted counterlungs, which are placed in the main rebreather housing, tend to have a higher work of breathing because they are positioned above the lungs when you're in the water. As mentioned a few times, gas in water rises. So gas in the rebreather loop will rise. Getting that gas back to a lower position requires a bit more effort. When you inhale through a rebreather loop, you are trying to pull the gas in the counterlungs down through the loop and into your lungs. Positioning the counterlungs directly over your lungs will provide the least amount of work of breathing in this configuration, but still increases it in comparison to other positions.

Counterlungs mounted on the chest, or over-the-shoulder counterlungs, as they are called, tend to have an easier work of breathing. In the over-the-shoulder configuration, they are positioned below the lungs but over the apices. With the counterlungs positioned below the lungs, inhalation is easier since the gas is rising up from the counterlungs rather than being pulled down.

With both rear mounted and over-the-shoulder positions, you have two counterlungs. One counterlung contains gas expelled from your lungs before it goes through the scrubber. The other counterlung contains fresh gas that has been scrubbed of carbon dioxide. This isn't the case with sidemounted rebreathers.

In sidemounted rebreathers, you have one counterlung in the cylindrical housing. There is no inspiratory side and expiratory side. The counterlung is typically the size of the cylinder, but the volume is reduced by the scrubber canister that is also inside of the cylinder. There is sufficient volume for the counterlung, but most of that is located at the bottom of the rebreather cylinder. When positioned on you, that places the usable volume of the counterlung adjacent to your hip, quite far from the lungs.

This doesn't mean decent work of breathing isn't possible from a sidemount rebreather. It means there's not much room for error in how the rebreather is positioned. To get decent work of breathing, the counterlung needs to be on the same plane as your lungs and the loop hoses. Altering this positioning affects the work of breathing. If you go into a head down position, the gas in the loop rises to the counterlung and inhalation becomes more difficult. If you go into a head up position, the gas in the counterlung rises to the loop hoses and your mouth, making it more difficult to exhale.

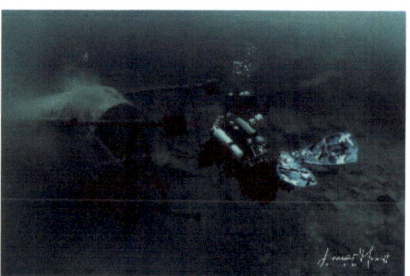

Backmount rebreather with rear mounted counterlungs positioned under the diluent and oxygen cylinders. This configuration requires air to be pulled down to your lungs increasing work of breathing.

Changes in orientation also affect rear mounted and over-the-shoulder counterlungs. However, the effect on work of breathing isn't as pronounced as it is with a single counterlung sidemounted rebreather. This is one of the reasons it is considered an advanced rebreather that should only be trained on once you have experience on a more traditional unit.

Another issue that arises with the use of sidemounted rebreathers is where to mount the diluent, oxygen, and bailout cylinders. Sidemount rebreathers, by design, are mounted at your side in place of one of your sidemount cylinders. The typical setup puts the diluent cylinder on the opposite side of the rebreather canister. You can continue using the same sidemount cylinder you normally use as long as you balance the weighting on both sides. Because the counterlung in the rebreather fills with gas when you exhale, it requires enough weight to counteract the positive buoyancy created by this. You also need an oxygen cylinder, but this is usually small enough to attach to the rebreather itself. There are even military spherical cylinders that can be attached to the bottom of the rebreather housing. You can expect to spend $3000 to $5000 USD just for the sphere and housing attachment.

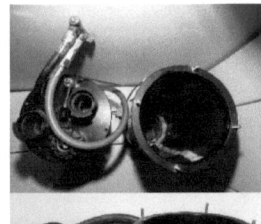

Sidemount rebreather with single counterlung surrounding the scrubber canister. The scrubber canister (left) takes up most of the room in the housing.

This leaves the bailout cylinder. Some divers choose to have the diluent cylinder play double duty and also be a bailout cylinder. If their rebreather fails, they bailout to a 2nd stage regulator on their diluent cylinder and end the dive. However, if you lose your diluent due to a 1st stage failure, you also lose your bailout gas. You can use an H valve to add a second 1st stage. If you don't do this, another cylinder should be used. If it's not, complete redundancy is not achieved, and that 1st stage failure could be fatal. Since the required amount of diluent isn't a large volume, it can be mounted to the rebreather itself. This would free up the sidemounted cylinder to serve strictly as bailout.

Ideally, the diluent cylinder is sidemounted on one side, and the rebreather on the other side with a small oxygen cylinder attached. If you don't opt to spend the money on a spherical oxygen cylinder, you can secure a small cylinder to the side of the housing so it rests nestled between the rebreather and your torso. You can then top or bottom mount an aluminum 80 cf/11 L cylinder in stage fashion for your bailout. That brings us into a more technical aspect of sidemount diving.

Another option is to sidemount a rebreather while backmounting a small twinset for bailout gas. This offers an alternative configuration that allows the diver to carry sufficient bailout gas throughout the dive. The rebreather setup is sidemounted with the rebreather and oxygen mounted on one side and the diluent on the other. The bailout is positioned on the back.

Chest mounted rebreathers have become more popular over recent years. The scrubber is mounted in front of the diver with the counterlungs housed inside of the unit. With this configuration, all you have to do is add the rebreather to the sidemount setup. One sidemount cylinder is classified as diluent and the other as bailout. Modifications will be minimal. Add a small oxygen cylinder, usually on the back, much like a dry suit inflation cylinder, and you're set.

There is a sidemount rebreather on the market that uses two counterlungs. It's not a true sidemount rebreather because the scrubber canisters are mounted on the back. However, it is designed to be used exclusively with a sidemount configuration. Rather than being directly on the back, the scrubber

Sidemount rebreather with oxygen cylinder at the top and diluent cylinder at the bottom both attached to the rebreather. The bailout cylinder is mounted on the opposite side of the diver.

Sidemount rebreather with black oxygen cylinder secured to the side of the rebreather and bailout in a small twinset on the back

Sidemount rebreather used with a twinset configuration. The counterlung is positioned between the arrows. A black oxygen cylinder is mounted above the rebreather housing.

True application of a sidemount rebreather. The rebreather is mounted on the right and the diluent is on the left. Oxygen is in a spherical cylinder located at the bottom of the rebreather. The diluent cylinder is also used as a bailout cylinder.

canisters are mounted above the sidemount cylinders in the valley created by the cylinders and the torso. The rebreather is designed to position the counterlungs next to the ribs over your lungs. The work of breathing on this rebreather is very minimal due to this positioning.

With this rebreather, sidemount cylinders are still used in standard configuration. One sidemount cylinder is designated as the diluent and the other one as the bailout. The scrubber canisters are mounted above the counterlungs, nestled into the space between the sidemount cylinders and your torso. The oxygen cylinder is mounted across the bottom of the rig on the rear, similar to a dry suit inflation cylinder (which may affect trim) or to the front of one of the sidemount cylinders.

Rebreathers are a tool. They have their place in diving, even recreational scuba diving, but they come with caveats. Keep this in mind. And remember, they may not be the best tool for all dives.

Sidemount rebreather with scrubber canister mounted above the sidemount cylinder being used as diluent. The other sidemount cylinder is designated as bailout. Oxygen cylinder is rear mounted.

14 SIDEMOUNT AND BOAT DIVING

Sidemount diving has grown more popular in the open water market. Because of this, dive boat operators have witnessed an increase in the number of sidemount divers on their boats. There certainly isn't a great revolution happening, but one of the more common questions by new sidemount divers is what it's like to sidemount from a boat. Another question addresses the special issues that should be taken into consideration when using sidemount when diving from a boat.

The first thing to take into account is whether the dive boat operation you are planning to dive with can or will accommodate sidemount divers. Because it's still not very common to see sidemount divers on boats, some captains aren't familiar with it and may not be willing to allow it, initially. This is where a little patience and an explanation might help.

A majority of dive charters cater to recreational divers. They run trips to local dive sites with the intent of getting two dives in before lunch so they can head out again after lunch. If they're not running boats with divers on them, they're not making money, so this makes sense. Because of this, most will limit bottom times in order to stay on schedule. When they hear a diver saying they want to dive with two cylinders, they get concerned about bottom times.

While one reason for this concern is the schedule, they may also be concerned about being compliant with their insurance policy. Some policies only cover recreational diving, and two cylinders means more bottom time, which in turn could mean decompression dives. At least, in their minds, it does. If you want to remain underwater longer, be honest and find a boat that's willing to accommodate you. There are plenty available. If you just want to dive sidemount to dive sidemount, then explain to them that you will comply with their time limits, and that you will not be staying beyond no decompression limits. And make sure you do that!

A great way to plan sidemount dives on two-tank dive charters is to end your first dive with 2000 psi/140 Bar in each cylinder. Then use the same cylinders for the second dive and end that dive with 1000 psi/70 Bar in each cylinder. That's the equivalent of breathing one cylinder to 1000 psi/70 Bar on each dive. If you explain this to the boat captain, you may have someone who is willing to accommodate your request. Just be sure you stick to the plan. If the dive time is limited to 45 minutes, be on the surface at 45 minutes. If you try to push the limits, not only will you likely not be allowed to return to dive from that boat, but you will also ruin it for other divers who want to dive sidemount and are willing to comply with the limits set by the captain.

Another concern in regards to boat diving is space. There may only be room at each station for one cylinder. While most trips are two-tank trips, the second cylinder may be stored elsewhere on the boat. They might be below the deck or in the cabin, and the crew pulls them out while you're on the first dive and stores the used cylinders when you return. If that's the case, ask the crew if you can have your second cylinder and keep it out of the way. If they agree, sling one cylinder onto

Preparing to splash into Lake Michigan, Chicago, Illinois, USA

Rotarian Wreck, Lake Michigan, Chicago, Illinois, USA

Wells Burt Wreck, Lake Michigan, Chicago, Illinois, USA

your side and have the second cylinder hanging on an equipment line in the water or in between your legs until it's your turn to splash. Then carry it with you and secure it to your rig once in the water. Make sure you talk to the crew to see what your options are. If they aren't willing to let you dive with two cylinders, see the next chapter.

That brings us to the next concern of boat diving – how to gear up. There are a couple ways to approach sidemount diving on a boat. You can don all of your gear while on the boat, if there's sufficient room, and enter the water completely geared up. Or you can drop your cylinders into the water on equipment lines and don them in the water. Either way works well, but sea conditions could dictate which works better at the time. Ultimately, the choice is yours based on what you are more comfortable with.

If the seas are flat, either method works. However, if the seas are a little rough, you'll have to weigh the advantages and disadvantages of gearing up on the boat versus gearing up in the water. If you gear up on the boat, you can do a negative entry, get to 20 feet/6 meters depth, and wait for the rest of the divers. However, getting from your spot on the boat to the entry point could prove challenging. It can be difficult enough with a single cylinder on your back. While having your cylinders hanging at your sides lowers your center of gravity and makes you somewhat more stable, you are heavier, and a rough wave can topple you over quickly.

If you gear up in the water, you don't have to be concerned about a rocking boat tossing you around as much. However, you will have to deal with floating on the surface while you secure the first cylinder to your rig enough to start breathing from it. Once the first cylinder is secured, you can grab the second cylinder from the equipment line and drop down to a comfortable depth to finish the process. Make sure you practice this in a safe environment before attempting it from a boat. You don't want to hold up the rest of the divers or the crew. And you don't want to accidently drop a cylinder and have to deal with trying to get it from the bottom. You could damage the reef or you may lose your cylinder because you're doing a wall dive and the bottom is deeper than recreational limits.

It's easy enough gearing up in sidemount when you can bring your cylinders to the water one at a time and stand in waist deep water to gear up. It's a completely different thing to do this on a boat or in the ocean while floating on the surface. The first thing you want to do is become proficient in donning your sidemount gear as if you were on a boat. Set up a bench similar to what you might find on a boat, and practice gearing up and walking a few steps. To gear up on the boat, don your rig as you would at any other time. Place your cylinders close to you and your station. If you have the room, laying them on their sides on the bench with the valves facing toward you is the best way to do this. It keeps the cylinders lying flat so they don't get knocked over, and you can reach down, grab the valve, and pull it up when you are ready to clip it on.

If there isn't enough room, you can lay the cylinders on the floor under the bench at your spot. You should have at least the width of two cylinders to work with on any dive boat. When you're ready to clip them on, reach down for one of the valves and stand it up in front of you. Depending on your height and the height of the bench, you may have to bend down slightly to clip or bungee the top of the cylinder to your rig. If you have the room, stand the cylinder on the bench where you would sit and lean into it to secure it to your rig. You can then clip the bottom bolt snap to your D-ring or rail.

Once the first cylinder is in place, bend down and grab the valve of the second cylinder and pull it up so it is standing. If you have room, stand it on the bench just behind you on the opposite side of the first cylinder and secure it to your rig. Once both cylinders are clipped on, you are ready to enter the water. This is where having leashes on the necks of the cylinders helps because they will support the weight of the cylinders as you're walking to the stern of the boat.

Put on your mask and walk to the water entry location on the boat. You can put your fins on at this time or jump in and put them on in the water. It may be easier to put them on in the water. Make sure your wing is inflated and able to float you if you jump in without fins because you won't be able to fin yourself up. If you are only able to secure one cylinder and are carrying the other cylinder, make sure to clip the second cylinder onto a D-ring, so if you lose your grasp of it, you don't drop it. This is another time that having a leash around the neck is helpful.

Before you try this on a boat, find a place to practice doing giant strides into a pool or from a dock. Practice it several times and at different points of donning your cylinders. Try it with both cylinders properly secured to your rig and fins on and off, with one cylinder secured to your rig and the other in your hand with fins on and off, and with the cylinders already in the water clipped to an equipment line. Become proficient in all configurations. Doing a giant stride with sidemount gear is different than with backmounted cylinders. Again, you don't want to be the one holding up the rest of the divers and crew.

Giant stride in full kit off a boat including having fins on. Leashes on the cylinder necks keep the cylinders from hanging lower.

If you prefer to put the cylinders on in the water, and the boat crew is agreeable, you can lower them into the water on equipment lines. At least one cylinder (the one you normally put on first) should be within reach of the surface. The other cylinder can hang at a depth of 10-20 feet/3-6 meters. This needs to be practiced while floating in the water in the deep side of a pool or in local quarry or lake before you try it on a boat. The key is to clip the cylinder to your shoulder D-ring as soon as you unclip it from the equipment line, route the 2nd stage to your mouth, and keep your face in the water as you attach the cylinder, hoses, and bungees. Once the first cylinder is on, you can descend to the other cylinder and do the same at depth.

The main reason you clip the cylinders at different depths is so that when you lower them down or pull them back up, you only have the dry weight of one of the cylinders on the line at a time. If both cylinders are clipped to the same loop on the line, they will both be out of the water at the same time and you'll be hoisting 90 lbs/42 kg. By spacing them on different loops, you clip on one cylinder, lower it to the water, then clip the second cylinder and lower it to the water. When pulling the line up, you reverse the order. The first cylinder comes out of the water for you to unclip while the second cylinder remains submerged and isn't exerting 45 lbs/21 kg of weight while you deal with the first cylinder.

You may even be able to do a seated entry from the boat. Again, that's completely up to the crew and what they are willing to allow. A

145

seated entry with sidemount cylinders is a little more difficult than doing it with a backmounted cylinder. As you rotate your back toward the water, you have to drag both cylinders around to get them off of the platform. Or you can just do a face plant, but I wouldn't recommend that.

Seated entry in sidemount

Practice these skills! If you don't practice, you'll end up wasting time while everyone else is diving. You'll miss most of the dive. Don't make the crew regret allowing you to dive sidemount from their boat. Be courteous and proficient. Once you are proficient, book that boat diving trip.

Getting out of the water back onto the boat can be just as simple. If using equipment lines, remove the cylinders from your rig one at a time and clip them onto the lines so you can pull them up once you're back on the boat. If the boat crew pulls them up for you, make sure you tip them well! Remember the recommendation on the previous page to position the second cylinder 10-20 feet/3-6 meters deep! The boat crew might even be willing to have you hand your cylinders up to them one at a time. If that's the case, be quick. Don't hold up a line of divers waiting to get to the ladder. Be careful if the seas are not flat. You don't want to spend a lot of time next to a rocking boat. This is when an equipment line is preferred. I'll say it again - tip the crew! If they're pulling your cylinders up, they're doing extra work. Reward them for that. They normally work only for tips.

Another option is to climb onto the boat with the cylinders secured to your sides. If you have ever done any boat diving with backmounted doubles, you may find you feel more stable on the boat ladder and deck in sidemount, especially in rougher seas. The mass of the weight has been moved from your back to your sides. This shifts the center of gravity to a lower point on your body. Rather than pulling you back, the weight is pulling you down and making you more stable.

You have to make sure it's possible to get on the boat you're diving from with the cylinders at your sides. If the ladder is narrow with rails on both sides, you will have to turn slightly sideways to fit between the rails. Usually the rails are only at the top of the ladder and you can step

Getting back on the boat in full kit. The ladder rails make it necessary to turn sideways.

up high enough to get over them. If the boat is equipped with a dive ladder, it will be much easier, but you still have to be aware of your surroundings. If you're diving from of a boat with an outboard motor and the dive ladder is next to the outboard, don't slam your cylinder into it. The covers are made of fiberglass and enough force from a cylinder can crack it. That will be an expensive mistake!

Once you're back on the boat, make sure you get your cylinders out of the way so they don't become obstacles for the other divers or the crew. Be courteous! Unclip the cylinders and tuck them out of the way in a tank rack or under your bench. Then wait until the boat relocates to the next dive site. While everyone else is swapping out cylinders, you're relaxing because you will be using the same cylinders on the next dive. As you would anytime on a boat, respect other divers and crew.

Anytime you're on the boat with your cylinders clipped on, be aware of your surroundings. Dive boats are designed for single backmounted cylinder divers. You may have benches in the center with cylinder racks on the outer perimeter or benches to the outside with racks in the center. The space between the benches and racks is usually only a couple of feet/60 cm. Even with one cylinder hanging from your side, it is more likely to come in contact with the bench or the rack, or cylinders and someone else's regulators in the rack. Be aware of that and avoid damaging the boat or someone else's gear.

If you still have reservations about diving sidemount from a boat, or encounter problems trying to find a boat that will allow you to sidemount two cylinders, check out the next chapter. That may be a better option.

15 MONKEY DIVING

One of the take offs from sidemount diving is monkey diving. Monkey diving is described as diving with one sidemounted cylinder rather than two. Some also include a dive propulsion vehicle in this description, but this isn't necessary for it to qualify. The origin of the phrase monkey diving isn't known. Maybe it's because you're monkeying around in this configuration. Moving the cylinder from your back to your side and ridding yourself of that weight gives you a great feeling of freedom. It's the closest thing to freediving, except with a cylinder.

The true form of monkey diving - diving with a harness and single cylinder, no wing. Buoyancy is controlled only by the lungs. The closest one can get to the freedom of free diving with the ability to remain underwater for much longer.

Not all dives require the redundancy of two cylinders. Some can easily be done with a single cylinder. As mentioned in the previous chapter, you might also encounter some dive boats that won't allow you to dive with two cylinders for one reason or another. If that's the case, why use two? Take one cylinder with you and enjoy the freedom of nothing on your back while appeasing the boat captain and crew. I've been diving from boats this way for years.

Once you begin diving sidemount, you may find that you prefer to not mount cylinders on your back. You can easily address this with a small modification to your regulators and diving with only one cylinder. You may not even need a buoyancy control bladder with a single cylinder. There is such a small shift in the buoyancy of an aluminum 80 cf/11 L cylinder that your lungs should be able to handle the changes. I've done entire dives no deeper than 25 feet/7.5 m using a harness and aluminum 80 cf/11 L cylinder while controlling my buoyancy with my lungs. Talk about freedom!

While monkey diving can be done with any cylinder, it's best done with an aluminum 80 cf/11 L cylinder. Steel cylinders tend to be too negatively buoyant and create the need to balance the rig with trim weight on the opposite side. Aluminum cylinders, however, are light enough that one can be sidemounted without causing a list, thus negating the need for trim weight. That's right. You don't need to place a weight on the opposite side from the cylinder. As I mentioned previously, aluminum 80 cf/11 L cylinders are light enough and have such a small shift in buoyancy when breathed that when sidemounting two of them, you can breathe one down completely without affecting your trim.

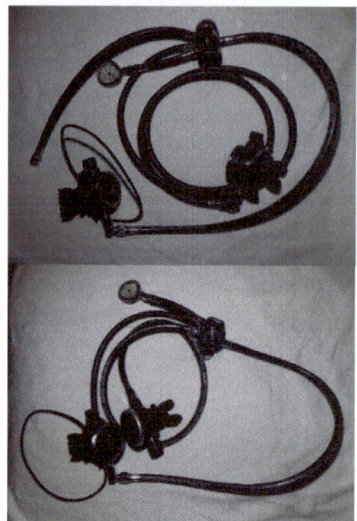

Monkey diving regulator setup. Top photo with 7 foot/2m long hose and bottom with 40 inch/100 cm long hose.

One modification you must do is to your regulators. You need to remove the 2nd stage and regulator hose from one of the 1st stages and add it to the other 1st stage. This will give you one 1st stage with two 2nd stages, an SPG, and a low pressure inflator hose. If you are monkey diving in a dry suit, you can either use the dry suit for buoyancy or move the low pressure inflator hose from the other 1st stage to the one you're using.

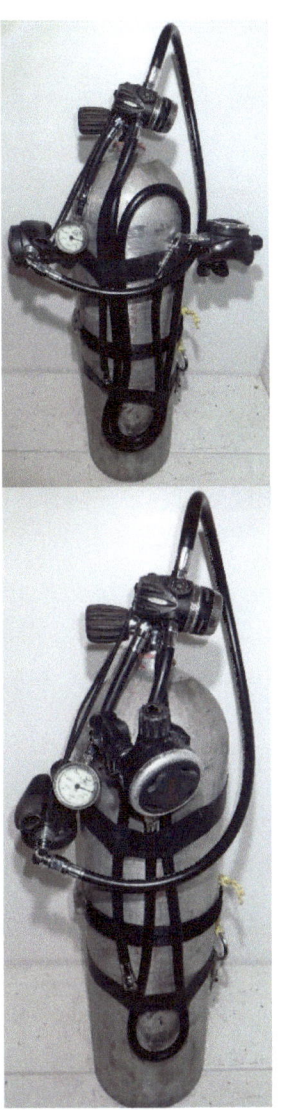

Monkey diving setup. Top cylinder with a 7 foot/2 m long hose. Bottom cylinder with 40 inch/100 cm long hose from a backmount setup.

This set up works best with a long hose and short hose combination. First, you'll be diving this configuration in a recreational setting with other recreational divers, so air sharing might be a possibility. You won't need to have both 2nd stages ready to use, though, because you won't be swapping regulators during the dive. If your sidemount setup is such that you use two short low pressure regulator hoses, you don't need to buy a 7 foot/2 m long hose just for monkey diving. Save the hose from your single cylinder backmount setup for this purpose.

The short hose 2nd stage will either route directly to your mouth or with the hose around your neck. The longer hose is secured on the cylinder with hose retainers. You can keep the 2nd stage secured to the cylinder as shown in photo to the left. Just know where it is, and build the muscle memory to be able to reach for it and deploy it without any thought. If you use a 7 foot/2 m long hose, the better option is to route the long hose around your neck and breathe from that regulator. If you need to donate, you can donate that 2nd stage regulator and switch to the other regulator, which should be on a necklace around your neck or clipped to a chest D-ring. If it's clipped to a D-ring, make sure it has a breakaway bolt snap on it to allow for quick access.

Why monkey dive at all? Why not just strap the cylinder to your back and dive in the traditional configuration? Monkey diving offers a more streamlined profile in the water. Because the cylinder is positioned in the armpit, a large portion of the cylinder is covered by the shoulder. There is less surface area to create drag as the diver swims through the water. It also allows the cylinder to be in a location where you can see the valve. And it keeps the valve from being directly behind your head, where you would be prevented from being able to bring your head back completely. Other than that, it can just be more comfortable and a lot more fun!

As with diving sidemount with two cylinders from a dive boat, make sure to talk to the captain and/or crew of the boat before you book the trip. Even with one cylinder, some boat crews don't want someone diving sidemount. This is usually because they haven't been exposed to it and don't understand it. Although, that's becoming less of an issue as sidemount becomes more popular. Most dive boat crews will be willing to accommodate sidemount divers, especially those monkey diving. I've only encountered one dive center in the past 20 years that was unwilling to accommodate sidemount divers on its boats. We simply found a different dive center that did accommodate us. With one dive boat that we did some monkey diving from, the only concern the captain had was chipping the new paint job. This is a valid concern because repairing chipped paint isn't as simple as doing a touchup. Marine paint must be used and most locations require inspections before and after.

Diving a reef in Grand Cayman while monkey diving. You can just see the cylinder on the diver's left side.

Monkey diving in Grand Cayman

Monkey diving in Grand Cayman

Chipped paint can also lead to rust from the salt water, and rust on a boat is never a good thing. So he wanted us to be careful that our cylinders didn't bang against the boat when getting in and out of the water. Other than that, we've gotten more curious stares and questions about our rigs and the way we dive than anything else. People are usually intrigued by what we're doing.

Play around with monkey diving at your local dive site. Get your rig and cylinder set up and comfortable. Then maybe next time you take a trip to some tropical diving location, you can experience the joy of monkey diving!

16 HISTORY OF SIDEMOUNT DIVING

We've spent the last 15 chapters discussing sidemount, different configurations within it, a variety of skills, and more. No discussion on sidemount is complete without taking a look at its origins. Why did divers find a need to remove cylinders from the back and mount them on the sides?

Sidemount diving has its origins in the United Kingdom. The United Kingdom is well known for its dry caves and the cave exploration that has taken place there. One of the most famous caves in the UK, Wookey Hole, is where one of the first known attempts at cave diving took place. In 1935, the Cave Diving Group, the oldest dive club in the world, conducted its first dive into Wookey Hole using equipment loaned by Siebe Gorman. The Cave Diving Group experimented with many different types of diving equipment, eventually bringing about the first sidemount rig.

Dry section of la Finou, The Lot, France

The first sidemount rig was very different from the rigs we currently see being commercially produced by dive equipment manufacturers. It consisted of a belt with a loop on each side designed to hold the cylinders on the body of the diver. The cylinders were positioned low on the body. The main advantage of this configuration was the simplicity of it. Cave explorers were more easily able to carry single cylinders, rather than manifolded cylinders, into the caves to the sumps where they would be needed. The cavers required smaller cylinders because of the need to carry them long distances through air-filled cave passages. They also didn't need as much air because the sumps were typically shallow and not very long. However, they did recognize the need for redundancy. Having two cylinders added the redundancy required by an overhead environment. The harness system also had to be small enough to be worn or carried in a small pack.

Le Lac, Cabouy, The Lot, France

As cave diving in the UK progressed, cave diving was also experiencing its beginnings in the United States. Florida, well known for the thousands of fresh water springs, was the center of cave diving activity. Quite a bit of cave exploration had taken place in many of the known springs. The passages that were explored were mainly large passages that could be negotiated by divers wearing backmounted double cylinders. This left miles of unexplored tunnels.

Woody Jasper, a Florida cave diver, had heard of the sidemount rigs being used in the UK and started developing his own system that would be useful for the type of diving he was doing in Florida. He eventually developed a system consisting of a recreational buoyancy compensator that could counteract the negative buoyancy of heavier steel cylinders. The larger steel cylinders required in the deeper water-filled passages of Florida caves were not so easily held in place by webbing on the hips of the divers. This led to a harness that was modified with hardware to hold the cylinders in place along the side of a diver's body. Some of the passages in Florida caves not only require the lower profile of sidemount, but also a narrower profile than sidemount could offer. This meant the cylinders had to be easily removed from the rig while underwater in order to be able to negotiate the smaller restrictions.

Over the years, sidemount systems have evolved significantly. Many divers created their own rigs in the early days out of necessity. Finally, in the late 1990s/early 2000s, the first couple of commercially available sidemount systems were produced and placed on the market – the Dive Rite Nomad and the Armadillo. While they shared many similar features, they also differed from each other in many ways, namely in the harness and the lift capacity of the wings. One was developed for the masses while the other was developed with the focus of exploration.

Diving sidemount in Curaçao

Diving sidemount in Curaçao

Getting ready to dive in Grand Cayman

Today, we have dozens upon dozens of commercially produced sidemount systems available to divers. At first, many of these systems were designed with the cave diver in mind, specifically the Florida cave diver. They were designed with a lot of lift for heavy steel cylinders. Part of the reason for the lift capacity is that there are still quite a few divers in Florida that dive the caves in wetsuits, so they need the added lift to counteract, not only the shift in cylinder buoyancy, but also the neoprene compression as they get deeper.

Some sidemount rigs were also being developed in another popular cave diving destination – the Yucatan Peninsula of Mexico. Because, at the time, the most common cylinders available for use were aluminum 80 cf/11 L cylinders, these rigs were developed specifically for that cylinder. Most of the caves in Mexico are very shallow, so the use of smaller cylinders allows for sufficiently long dives.

Limiting a product to such a narrow market doesn't generate much in sales. Both sides of the spectrum began looking at what modifications they could make to their products so they would appeal to both markets – those diving steel cylinders and those diving aluminum cylinders. This resulted in the manufacturers of what was commonly known as Florida rigs to create smaller rigs and the manufacturers of the Mexico rigs to add wings with more lift to appeal to the steel cylinder customer.

As sidemount started gaining popularity among recreational divers, this opened up a new field. Sidemount rigs that are better suited to open water diving were introduced to the market. Most sidemount rigs today are marketed to all divers. Manufacturers are trying to appeal to everyone with the one or two rigs that they sell. We now have so many options for new sidemount divers that it can be overwhelming when trying to decide which rig to purchase. Many people dive these systems without modification out of the bag. Many modify these systems to suit their diving.

Diving sidemount in Bonaire

The evolution is not over. Sidemount systems continue to evolve as more and more divers experiment with this type of diving. Unlike traditional Hogarthian backmount systems, there will likely never be a standard sidemount configuration that is accepted by a majority of sidemount divers. While most divers begin diving manifolded backmounted double cylinders for a specific purpose, such as technical diving, divers begin sidemount diving for a variety of purposes. As long as this holds true, a standard rig will never be developed.

Diving sidemount in Grand Cayman

Penetrating the C-53 wreck in Cozumel, Mexico

17 BUILDING YOUR OWN SIDEMOUNT RIG

With all of the commercially available sidemount systems on the market today, why would anyone need or want to build their own sidemount rig? Well, divers tend to like to tinker. We like to build things using parts bought at hardware stores. I've seen a rebreather that was built from PVC pipe! Even with so many options available, sometimes building something of your own so it meets your exact specifications may be the best option. And it can be rewarding.

There are also some people who want to try sidemount but don't want to put the money into a manufactured rig. While they can easily do this by scheduling a day with an instructor that has several sidemount rigs available for a sidemount experience, they prefer to spend hours looking at photos of manufactured rigs and trying to duplicate them the best that they can at home. There's nothing wrong with building your own rig, but it's rather difficult to build a piece of equipment to use for something you've never done. In order to build an effective sidemount rig, you need to understand sidemount diving from the perspective of a sidemount diver. The only way to do that is to become a sidemount diver. This is why this chapter is the last one in this book. You should build your experience as a sidemount diver before you attempt to build your own sidemount rig. My first experience in a sidemount rig was in one I built from a harness and wing I already had. While I enjoyed the experience, the rig was not at all streamlined. Back then, there weren't many options, though. There were two commercially available sidemount rigs, very few sidemount instructors, and only one agency offering a sidemount course at that time.

Early divers built sidemount rigs from simple web harnesses and collar buoyancy compensators. The rigs were designed to hold the cylinders at the side, next to the hips (much lower than in later designs). It was a simple, streamlined design. However, the cylinders used at the time were small and had little effect on the diver's trim. Those rigs also had limited use, primarily used to get past sumps in dry caves.

Florida cave divers took early sump diver designs and expanded upon them to suit their needs. Jacket buoyancy compensator devices (BCDs) were modified by removing cam bands from the rear of the device, adding bicycle inner tube to hold the cylinder valves in place, and adding a harness with D-rings to clip the cylinder bottoms. Some divers still use this style of rig and claim there is an advantage to having the lift around the entire body rather than on the back of the diver. Recall the discussion about spreading the lift around? There's something to that.

These are simple rigs to build. Jacket BCDs are easy to come by in any number of used gear marketplaces. A separate harness is then made and worn beneath the jacket BCD. Bungees for the cylinder valves are attached to the harness. If you want to go old school, a bicycle innertube can be routed through the slots for the cam straps and used to hold the valves. One of these rigs can be made for about $100 USD quite easily. While they served their purpose in the early days, they have limitations and shouldn't be the type of rig you strive to build and dive.

Traditional cave diving rigs consist of a hard back plate and wing. Naturally, some early sidemount divers experimented with similar designs. There are divers who still use

Stab jacket buoyancy compensator modified for sidemount. A harness is worn inside the jacket to provide a way to secure cylinders and add stability to the rig. The jacket BCD only serves to control buoyancy.

Manufactured harness over a single cylinder wing

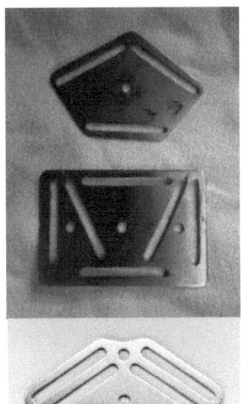

that design by sandwiching the wing between two back plates (see chapter 2). This was done to provide a way to add weight to a versatile rig that can be used for multiple configurations. If you don't need the additional weight of the backplates, or you want flexibility along your back, you can use a soft harness instead. These can be purchased pre-made or constructed easily.

If you have looked at a variety of sidemount systems that use horseshoe or donut shaped wings with separate harnesses, a common thing you should have noticed is that the wing is positioned under the harness. This allows the harness to hold the wing down wherever it crosses over it. While this holds a portion of the wing down, there are areas where the edges of the wing taco up when it has air in it. Bungees under the wing help to prevent this, but they only do so much to pull the wing down because they are routed from the outside of the wing to the inside. Another option is to have tabs sewn into the wing to secure a belly band.

Different types of harnesses can be used or built for a sidemount rig. Pretty much any soft harness can be placed over most wings. This may work without further modification or may require additional tabs to hold the edges of the wing down. A harness can also be built using 2 inch/5 cm webbing. There are several sources for stainless steel hardware that is designed to be used in harnesses, and more specifically to be used with sidemount harnesses. If you have access to a machine shop, you can also create your own. If you want something a little more permanent, you can sew the webbing rather than use plates (an industrial sewing machine is handy in this situation - see your local shoe repair shop). You can also burn a hole through the webbing where it crosses and use sex bolts to hold the webbing together. This will not be as durable as the other options, but is an inexpensive way to throw something together to try in the pool or open water. Be creative. That's how we have gotten so many options available to us.

If you decide to build your harness, you need to decide whether you want an H harness or a V harness. Once that's decided, you'll need to get the following items:

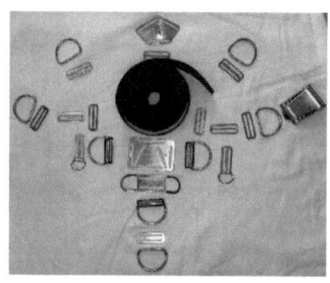

Typical hardware required to build a sidemount harness

- About 20 feet/6 m of 2 inch/5 cm webbing
- Sidemount hardware plates (the triangle shaped shoulder plate and the rectangle shaped lumbar plate pictured on the previous page)
- At least 9 triglides for a V harness, 13 for an H harness
- At least 8 D-rings
- Buckle

There is hardware that is specifically made for sidemount that can be used in place of the triglides and D-rings. Those tend to be a little more expensive, but if you are all in, I recommend using those. You can also add D-rings, including offset D-rings, but this list will get you started with the most basic harness. Start with the spine and crotch strap of the rig. (See appendices B, C, and D for step by step instructions with photos.)

First, insert the webbing through one slot of a triglide and then back through the other one, leaving it loose. Feed the webbing through the bottom slot of the shoulder plate. Fold the webbing over

Crotch strap loop created by a triglide and D-ring. This is initially placed about 12 inches/30 cm from the end. Then the loop is created. Note the opening of the loop is slightly larger than the webbing to allow the webbing to easily slide through.

and secure the loose end back through the triglide so the shoulder plate is secured to the loop you created. Tighten the webbing onto the triglide. Insert the other end of the webbing through the top slot of the lumbar plate and back through the bottom slot so that the lumbar plate is about 18 inches/45 cm from the shoulder plate.

Have someone hold the shoulder plate between your shoulder blades and slide the lumbar plate so that it is below your waist. Pull the excess webbing between your legs to your chest. Mark the webbing where it meets the bottom of your sternum. Cut the webbing at this location. Feed a triglide with D-ring onto the crotch strap so that it is positioned about 2 inches/5 cm below the lumbar plate. Feed a second triglide and D-ring onto the crotch strap and position it about 12 inches/30 cm from the end. Fold the end over to the inside, forming a loop about 3 inches/8 cm long, and feed the end through the triglide.

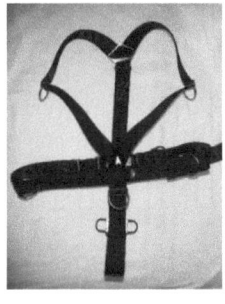

Completed V harness. The lumbar plate is the central point of focus for this harness with the shoulder plate securing the other end of the shoulder straps.

The next step is to make the shoulder straps. If you decided to make a V harness, you will feed one end of the remaining webbing pieces through one of the angled slots on the shoulder plate. Pull the webbing through so that the shoulder plate is centered. Feed a triglide and D-ring onto the top end of the webbing and position it about 12 inches/30 cm from the shoulder plate. This will be a chest D-ring. Add a second, if you desire. Fold the webbing over and feed the end without a D-ring through the other angled slot of the shoulder plate so that the fold is on the inside of the harness. Take the long end of the webbing with the D-ring and bring it up toward the front and back down to the lumbar plate. Feed it from the inside through the angled slot and back into the vertical slot. This forms the first shoulder strap. The remainder of the webbing forms one side of the waist strap. Make sure the webbing is twisted correctly. It will need to rotate inward so that the side facing in at the lumbar plate is also facing in at the shoulder plate.

Now repeat the process for the opposite side to form the other shoulder strap. I recommend adding triglides to the waist strap placed against the lumbar plate. This will prevent the webbing from shifting, resulting in uneven shoulder straps. Add waist D-rings, including offset D-rings, if desired, and finish it off with the buckle.

Put the harness on and adjust for sizing, keeping in mind that you'll need room for whatever exposure protection you typically wear on your dives. Be prepared to have to take it apart and rotate the shoulder straps so that they are correct and the D-rings are facing out. You're bound to make a mistake on at least one side!

If you decided to make an H harness, the process is slightly easier and less confusing. After creating the spine and crotch strap, feed the webbing you have left through the vertical slots of the lumbar plate enough for one end to route from the lumbar plate around your waist and across to the opposite hip. Mark and cut the other side of the webbing so that it is the same length. This is the waist strap. Place rear and side D-rings on each side as desired.

H harness – the lumbar plate only stabilizes the waist, spine, and crotch straps. The shoulder straps are secured to the shoulder plate and the front of the waist strap.

Take the remaining section of webbing and feed it through the shoulder plate with the fold on the inside as previously described, leaving equal lengths of webbing on each side. Place chest D-rings as desired. Place a triglide on each shoulder strap about 12 inches/30 cm below the lowest chest D-ring. Form a loop measuring 2 ¼ inches/6 cm on each end, and feed it back through the triglide. Add front D-rings to each side of the waist strap, and slide the loops over the waist strap so they are positioned against the triglide and D-rings. Keep the loops from sliding on the waist strap by placing another triglide to the inside of each one. You can also add D-rings to these, if desired. Finish it off with a buckle. A simpler, yet more expensive way to attach the shoulder straps to the waist strap is by using the hardware mentioned above.

Put the harness on and adjust for sizing, keeping in mind exposure protection. With the H harness, you're unlikely to have to take it apart as there aren't any twists in the webbing.

Now you need to choose a wing for your harness. There are a variety of options available for the buoyancy compensator of the homemade system. An old jacket BC can be used. You'll still need a harness to wear with it so that you have D-rings because most jacket BCs don't come with D-rings in the right places for sidemount, if at all. And they aren't stable enough to hold heavier cylinders.

A wing designed for backmount can also be modified to work with a sidemount system. Placing the harness over it will hold the top and bottom of the wing down. You will need to figure out a way to secure the sides to keep them from lifting up. Belly bands work best, if you can secure them to the middle of the wing. The lift will be evenly distributed along the length of the wing rather than concentrated at the bottom of the wing.

MSR bag with additional opening so it can be used as a wing

MSR bags can also be used for buoyancy control. The openings to the bags are typically the same size and threading as those of diving wings. However, MSR bags usually only have one opening rather than the two required for use as a buoyancy compensator. They should have a tube that can be used for oral inflation. There are some manufacturers that have developed MSR style sidemount wings. While an MSR bag may work well for sidemounting 80 cf/11 L cylinders, it will usually not provide sufficient lift for steel cylinders and will not remain flat when fully inflated.

There are a few options available that have been specifically designed for sidemount. A range of lift is available as well as grommets positioned along the perimeter to help secure the wing to the harness to maintain a low profile. One thing to look for when considering a wing, especially if you are looking at pillow shaped wings, is the presence of baffles. Baffles will help the wing maintain a lower profile rather than blowing up like a ball. Baffles that run vertically along the wing will be more effective than ones that are horizontally oriented.

The next thing to consider is how you will keep the cylinders in the proper position. Regardless of whether you want to use a bicycle innertube, loop bungees, straight bungees, ring bungees, or some other method, you need to have a way to attach them to your rig and keep them in place. The tube or bungee also needs to remain accessible once you put the rig on. If you do not have an attachment point to the front of the rig, the end of the tube or loop bungee can get caught in between you and your rig and you might not be able to reach it without assistance.

Bungee is the most common and effective means to keep the valves in the proper position in the armpits. Secure the bungee to the shoulder plate or the triglide that's positioned just under the shoulder plate. Some shoulder plates come with holes that are meant to be used to secure the bungee. If you choose to use loop bungees, form the loops and feed the folded end through the holes or through the triglide. Then secure the front to one of the D-rings using quick links and bolt snaps or static line. You might even be able to secure the rear of the bungees to your wing, depending on which wing you choose.

Finally, you need to keep the bottom of the cylinders attached to your rig. You can choose to use a butt plate, or attach them to offset D-rings coming off your

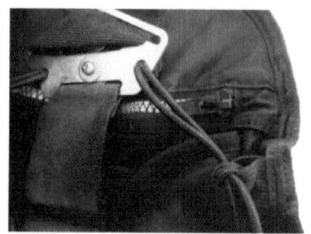

Bungee secured to shoulder plate

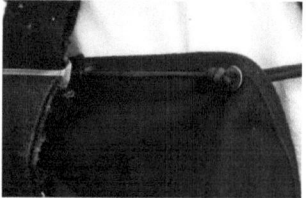

Bungee secured to harness and wing. The bungee routes through a grommet and has a knot to keep the wing stretched when inflated.

Bungee loop plate

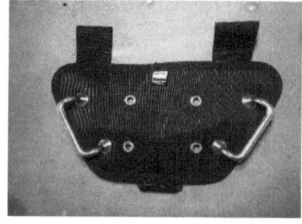

After market butt plates can be added to most sidemount rigs.

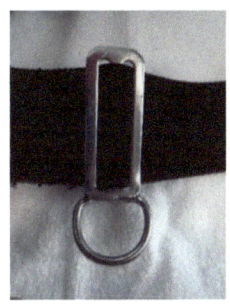

Offset D-ring

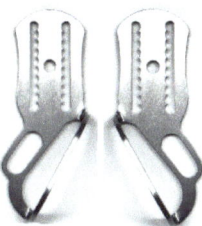

Drop D-rings

crotch strap or D-rings positioned on your waist strap. The determinants of what method will work best will be the buoyancy characteristics of the cylinders you will dive with that rig and the size of the wing you choose to use. If the wing extends down over the waist strap, you won't be able to reach D-rings on the waist strap, so that option won't work without drop D-rings.

The final decision you'll need to make regarding a sidemount rig using a pillow shaped wing is whether you mount the wing on top of the harness or underneath it. Most commercial sidemount systems come with the pillow shaped wing on top of the harness. This allows the wing to fully expand without being encumbered by the harness. However, this also creates a larger profile. By placing the wing under the harness, the spine strap provides resistance along the center and keeps the wing flatter. You do lose some of the lift capacity of the wing by doing this. You likely won't need the full lift capacity of the larger wings anyway.

It doesn't matter how you build your sidemount rig. What's important is to know what you are going to use it for and build it with that in mind. Make sure you have designed a way to keep the buoyancy bladder against your body and the entire rig as streamlined as possible. Get photos or video of yourself in the water with the rig on so you can see what it looks like. Just because it feels good in the water doesn't mean it looks good.

Wing mounted under harness

Don't forget to check out the appendix section for detailed steps with photos describing how to build both a V harness and an H harness.

IN SUMMARY

A lot of information has been covered in the last 17 chapters. We've discussed why divers choose to dive sidemount. If you were merely curious about sidemount before beginning this adventure, hopefully reading this book helped you decide why sidemount may be for you. While there is a lot of specific information that could be covered in regards to choosing a sidemount rig, there are too many choices and not enough space in this book for that. The best way to figure out which one works for you is to find divers that do the type of diving you want to do and question them about their sidemount systems and why they chose them. Ask them if you can try their systems in the water. Keep in mind that their sidemount rigs should be adjusted and modified to work for them and might not work so well for you. They might not want you to make adjustments to their rigs. Respect that, as you'll soon find out, it takes a lot of work to get those adjustments tuned in. Make sure you also try a variety of sidemount cylinders. You won't know what brand and size works best for you until you try a few different cylinders.

We finally moved into customizing sidemount systems so that they work optimally for you. Sidemount is too personalized to be able to just take a rig and start diving it. Changes must be made to get you in proper trim. Once you are trim in your sidemount rig, the basic skills of sidemount become much easier to do because you won't have to think about staying trim. The sidemount rig keeps you there. If you find yourself struggling to hold position in the water, then you haven't optimized your rig. Keep working on it!

We wrapped up the final chapters examining some specialty areas in sidemount – rebreathers, diving from boats, and monkey diving. Before you think about moving into any of these areas, build your experience in sidemount. Build your experience with a traditional rebreather. Then start looking at the sidemount rebreathers. Remember, none of the information presented here is a substitution for getting in the water and building experience.

One major difference between sidemount diving and backmount diving is donning. With backmount configuration, you set up the gear while it sits on a bench or table and then put the rig and cylinders on. With sidemount, the cylinders don't go on until after the rig is on. For the inexperienced sidemount diver, this is one of the most challenging areas. Until you've practiced it over and over, donning sidemount cylinders can be difficult and time consuming. You may find your buddies waiting on you while you struggle with it the first several times. That's why I keep repeating that you need to get in the water and practice before you get out there and dive in groups, especially from a boat. Build the muscle memory and proficiency in a pool or shallow quarry or lake. Get in the water and put the gear on and take it off until it's easy. Then go out there and enjoy it.

Sidemount is a fun way to dive. It provides a sense of freedom you don't experience in backmount. It provides more stability and flexibility. Sidemount can be whatever you want it to be. Even now, it's still a new enough discipline that established norms don't exist. That's one of the things that makes it fun.

Go out there and have fun! And above all, Dive Safe!

APPENDIX A – ATTACHING WEIGHTS WITH BUNGEES

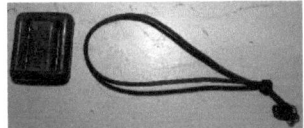

1. You will need a hard weight and 3/16 inch/5 mm bungee.

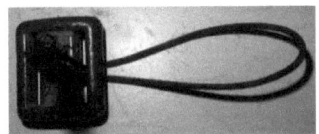

2. Insert the loop end down through one slot of the weight.

3. Wrap the loop around the webbing so the weight sits on top of the webbing.

4. Note the proper routing of the bungee through the weight and around the webbing.

5. Feed the loop back up through the other slot of the weight. Front and rear view of bungee around webbing and in both slots.

6. Pull the loop end across the weight and over the edge.
Finally, pull the knotted end across the other side of the weight and over the edge.

7. You now have a secure weight on your harness.

APPENDIX B – SPINE & CROTCH STRAP

1. Start with webbing that measures from the bottom of the back of your neck, down between your legs, and back up to your sternum. Secure webbing to bottom slot of shoulder plate using a triglide.

2. Insert through one slot of the triglide and back through the other slot. Insert the webbing through the bottom slot of the shoulder plate then feed it back through the triglide going up through the last slot the webbing came out of and back through the other slot. This part will be a little difficult with new, stiff webbing.

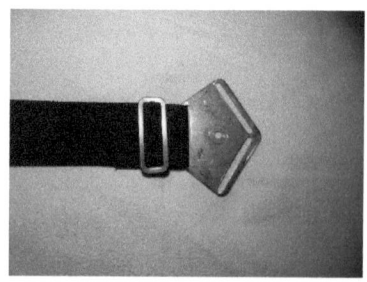

3. Tighten the webbing so the shoulder plate is only about 1 inch/2.5 cm from the triglide.

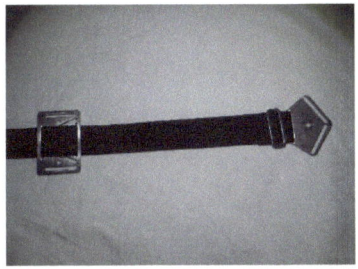

4. Insert the other end of the webbing through the top slot of the lumbar plate and back through the bottom slot of the plate, as shown.

5. Feed a rear D-ring onto the webbing about 8 inches/20 cm below the waist strap. This will be adjusted once the harness is complete. You have the option of using offset D-rings

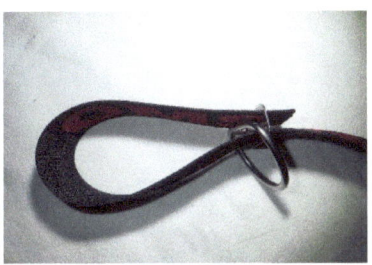

6. Feed the free end of the webbing through the slots of a triglide with a D-ring in between as shown. This will be the forward crotch D-ring.

7.Feed the free end up through the last slot the webbing came out of, around the D-ring, and back through the other slot.

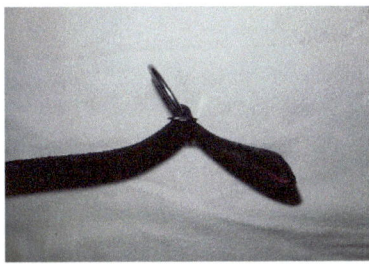

8. Tighten the webbing so the triglide and D-ring are positioned about 2.5 inches/3 cm from the end of the loop.

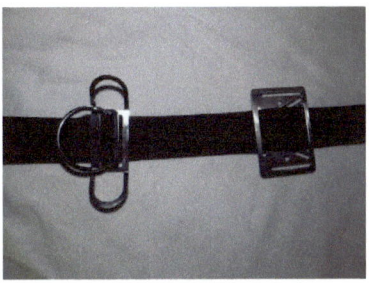

9. You will adjust the length of the crotch strap once the harness is complete.

Completed spine and crotch strap portion of both V and H harness

APPENDIX C – V HARNESS SHOULDER & WAIST

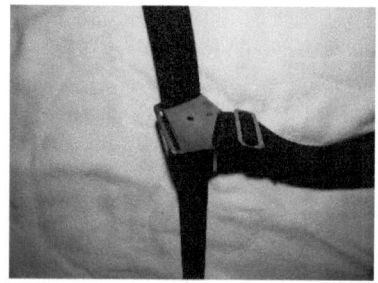

1. Insert one end of the remaining webbing through one of the angled slots in the shoulder plate. Center the plate on the webbing.

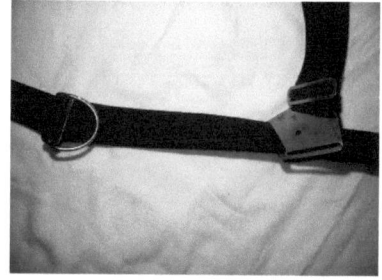

2. Feed a triglide and D-ring from the top end of the webbing and position it about 1 foot/30 cm from the shoulder plate. This will be a chest D-ring.

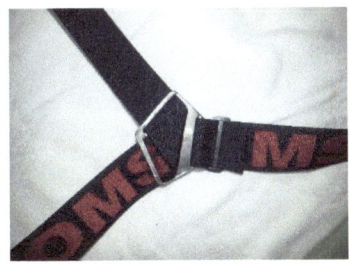

3. Fold the webbing over and feed the other end through the other angled slot so it looks as pictured. The fold will be on the inside of the plate when the harness is on.

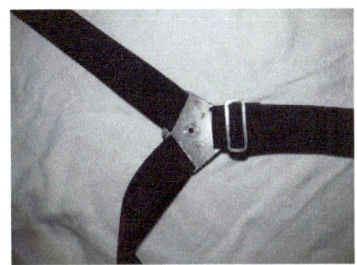

4. Reverse view of shoulder plate with webbing properly routed.

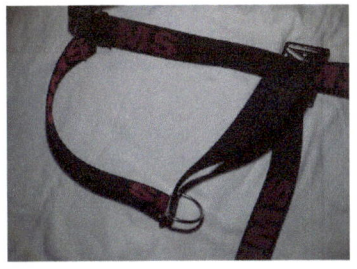

6. Feed the webbing back through the end slot to form one side of the waist band.

5. Feed the free end of the webbing with the D-ring through the slanted slot of the waist strap on the same side as the shoulder plate. The side of the webbing to the outside at the shoulder plate must be to the outside of the band.

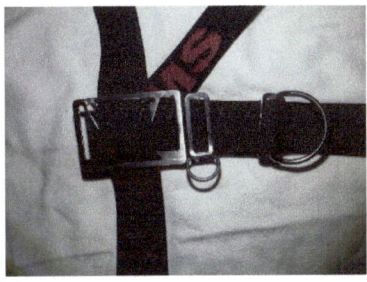

8. Feed a triglide & D-ring onto the webbing & position about 6 inches/15 cm from the lumbar plate. You can also place an offset D-ring next to the lumbar plate before placing the D-ring on the webbing. At minimum a triglide should go here to prevent sliding.

7. Reverse view of lumbar plate with webbing properly routed.

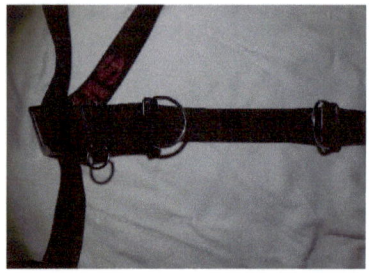

9. Feed another triglide and D-ring onto the webbing and position about a foot/30 cm from the first D-ring.

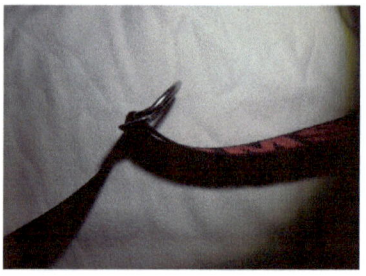

10. Feed a triglide and D-ring onto the other shoulder strap.

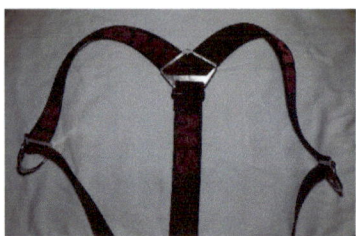

11. Position the D-ring even with the other side. These will be adjusted once the harness is completed.

12. Feed the end of the webbing through the slanted slot in the lumbar plate. The side of the webbing to the outside of the shoulder plate must be to the outside of the lumbar plate. Feed the webbing back through the straight slot.

13. Feed the hardware you will use on the other side of the waist strap – rear D-ring being required and offset D-ring optional. A triglide in this position prevents the webbing from sliding through the slots causing the shoulder straps to be uneven.

14. View of rear and offset D-rings.

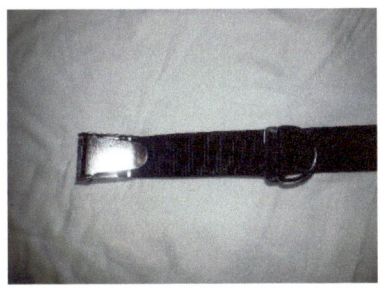

15. Feed the front D-ring onto the webbing. Finish off this side with a stainless steel buckle of your choice.

*Completed V Harness
Sidemount Rig*

APPENDIX D – H HARNESS SHOULDER & WAIST

1. Cut a length of webbing long enough to wrap around your waist plus an additional 1 foot/30 cm or longer. Feed the webbing through the lumbar plate slots, both straight and angled, as shown.

2. Feed the rear and offset D-rings onto one side of the webbing. The offset D-ring is optional. If you choose not to use it, a triglide in its place is helpful to keep the waist strap from sliding back and forth in the lumbar plate.

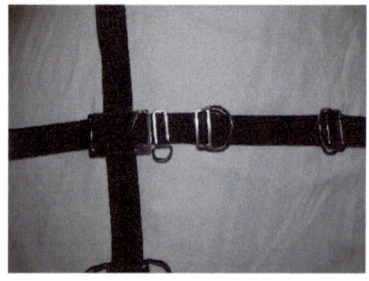

3. Feed the front D-ring onto the webbing so it is positioned about 1 foot/30 cm from the rear D-ring.

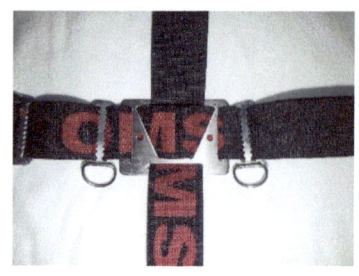

4. Set up the opposite side of the waist strap the same as you did the first side.

5. View of the lumbar plate with the waist strap in place. Substitute triglides for the offset D-rings if you choose.

6. Rear D-rings in place on the waist strap. These will be adjusted to the correct location once the harness is complete.

7. Completed waist strap with rear and front D-rings in place. They will be adjusted when the harness is complete.

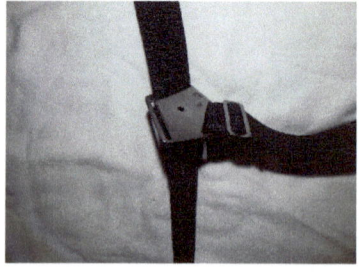

8. Feed the remaining webbing through the shoulder plate angled slot so the center of the webbing is at the plate.

9. Fold the webbing over and insert the other end through the angled slot on the other side of the shoulder plate as shown in the photo. This is the inside view.

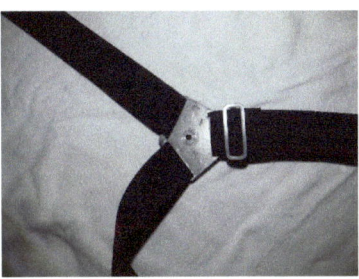

10. View of shoulder straps on shoulder plate. This is what will be seen from the back when the harness is on.

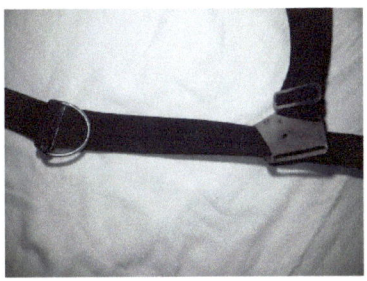

11. Feed a triglide and D-ring on one side of the webbing about 1 foot/30 cm from the shoulder plate.

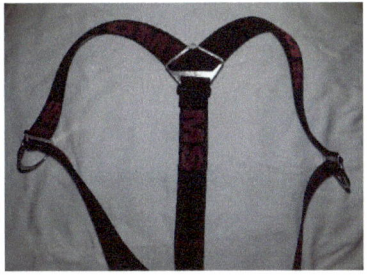

12. Feed a second triglide and D-ring on the other side of the webbing about 1 foot/30 cm from the shoulder plate. These are the chest D-rings.

13. Place a triglide on the ends of the shoulder strap webbing and create a loop on each end. Make the loop just big enough to slide the waist strap into it and crease the end of the loop.

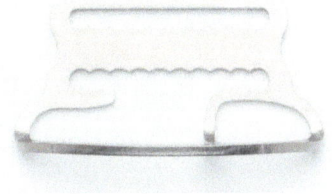

14. Specialty hardware, such as this, can be used in place of the triglides and D-rings shown in the images.

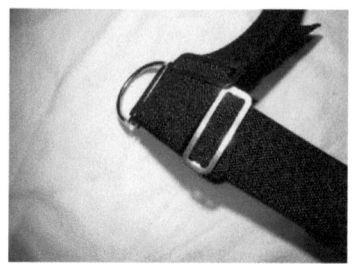

15. Slide the loop onto the waist strap against the front D-ring and place another triglide on the other side of the loop to hold it in place. The loop must be small enough to not be able to slide over the triglide.

16. This is what it should look like from the front. Repeat these steps for the other side. You can use a second D-ring here if needed.

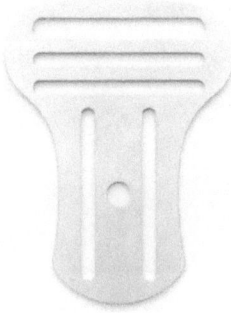

17. Specialty hardware is now available that can be used to secure the shoulder straps to the waist strap without the loops.

Completed H Harness Sidemount Rig

Completed H Harness Sidemount Rig with 22 lb/10 kg lift wing attached under the harness. Left – rear view / Right - front view

Index

Photo Index

Photo Credits

All photos by Rob Neto except those noted below

Concave cylinders, Choker & Ring bungee, Backmount style hose routing, Breakaway clip, Ring bungee in use, Checking stage SPG/Static line hanging, Accessing thigh pocket – Oliver Albrecht	27, 30, 43, 50, 59, 64, 119
T-S Sidemount System – www.toddy-style.com with permission of Toddy Waelde	18
LP hoses coming off 5th port – Kelly Koesis	38
Chapter 13, 16, 17 chapter photos – Laurent Miroult	132, 154, 160
SPG positioned below, swivel vs no swivel, rear mounted pouch, backmount rebreather, rebreather photos, true application of sidemount rebreather, dry cave photos, divers swimming away – Laurent Miroult	37, 50, 128, 136, 137, 138, 155, 156, 159, 172
Black aluminum bailout – Doug Ebersole	134
Boat diving in sidemount – Mike Pedersen	142, 145-147

ABOUT THE AUTHOR

Rob Neto has been sidemount diving since the mid-2000s. He began diving sidemount while living in Arizona after having seen it during one of his cave diving trips to Florida. He was intrigued with it and built his first sidemount rig from a single tank harness and wing he had and went diving. Like everything else he has done with diving, he became obsessed. Over the years he has experimented with various methods and sidemount rigs and currently uses three different sidemount rigs depending on the diving he is doing.

Rob currently lives in Greenwood, Florida, located in Jackson County, just minutes from some of the best cave diving in Florida. He dives sidemount exclusively even when traveling on recreational dive trips. He is an avid cave diver and cave explorer. He has done exploration in Florida, Mexico, and France and is currently active in several projects. Much of the exploration he does involves sidemount cave passage and he has even broken a stainless steel belt buckle going through a small, two bottle off restriction!

Rob has extensive experience diving both steel and aluminum cylinders, using multiple stage cylinders, and sidemounting his rebreather bailout cylinders. He taught sidemount, cave diving, and technical diving for more than 10 years before retiring to focus on cave exploration and enjoying life. Rob is the author of the *Beyond* thriller series and two true adventure series about his cave diving explorations in Florida and Cozumel, Mexico. His books can be ordered on his website, as well as any number of online retailers.

Litjåga Cave, Arctic Circle, Norway